THE ANSWER: GOD'S COVENANTS OF PROMISE

What All People Need to Know

John E. Hollywell

WESTBOW
PRESS®
A DIVISION OF THOMAS NELSON
& ZONDERVAN

WestBow Press books may be ordered through booksellers or by contacting:

WestBow Press
A Division of Thomas Nelson & Zondervan
1663 Liberty Drive
Bloomington, IN 47403
www.westbowpress.com
1 (866) 928-1240

ISBN: 978-1-5127-1300-8 (sc)
ISBN: 978-1-5127-1301-5 (hc)
ISBN: 978-1-5127-1299-5 (e)

Library of Congress Control Number: 2015915308

Print information available on the last page.

WestBow Press rev. date: 12/07/2015

CONTENTS

ABOUT THE AUTHOR

My name is John Hollywell. I was born in Liverpool in 1952. I came from a difficult background, and by the time I reached my teenage years, I was involved in the football hooligan Gangs of Liverpool FC. However, I had a praying Christian grandmother who, in the 1970s, petitioned the Lord for me daily. I always had a burning desire for answers to life's questions, such as Where did we come from? Why are we here? Where are we going in regards to eternity?

By 1979 I was taught astronomy and physics at Liverpool Museum and was given the position of Planetarium Operator, guiding and informing three audiences of seventy people a day and responding to their questions after each performance.

I met Jesus at the 1984 Billy Graham Crusade at Anfield in Liverpool and from then on studied God's word diligently four hours each day. I was prompted by the Lord to write this book.

MESSAGE TO THE READERS

First I encourage you to turn to the back cover and read about the author.

After many years of study, under instruction from anointed teachers of God's covenant promises (named in the author's dedication), I soon realized most people – both believers in Jesus and unbelievers –in the main had never heard explained accurately just what an awesome inheritance gift has been left to them as believers or what could be theirs if they asked Jesus to be their Lord and Saviour. Most people I met had questions that were never accurately and clearly answered in a way that they, as either believers or unbelievers, could easily understand.

Firstly, what is the Bible's explanation of why there is so much evil and chaos on the earth!

Secondly, what about so-called scientific answers to the same questions? And thirdly, why do governments, politicians, educational leaders, etc., have no explanation for widespread poverty, crime, war, disease, mental health problems, and depression? Finally, and most important, are there any answers that are guaranteed to solve one's problems and troubles, no matter how big or small, minor or serious?

The answer is yes, absolutely! The answers are found in a God/Man named Jesus Christ and in what He, the Creator of all things, including the earth and galactic universe, has promised to all who will invite this God/Man, Jesus, to come live in them and save them (from the soon-coming Tribulation on earth and from the Second Death – hell itself).

This book is the answer – read it!

—John Edward Hollywell

DEDICATION

I want to dedicate this book firstly to my Heavenly Dad and Father; to our Saviour and Lord, Jesus Christ; and to His Holy Spirit, who revealed to me His truths in a clear and awesome way.

Secondly, to my wonderful wife Lilian Ann, a beautiful woman and the one who helped me in all areas of my ministry with the sacrifice of both her time and her finances to help me write this book. For all her help with our ministry to the poor and in teaching groups in our home. What more could I say but "I love you, Lilian. Thank you!"

For our two sons, Michael and Jonathan, and daughter, Susanne, I thank God.

Much love to Brian and Sue Lord, my friends and fellow Bible college graduates; Steve and Lesley Mills, my mentor, and editors and friends.

For my grandma, Ena, for a lifetime of prayer for me.

And for my many teacher–scholars in Hebrew, Greek, and Scripture.

INTRODUCTION

The intent of this book is that your eyes will opened to see the Word of God as it was meant to be understood by all people, to see why seemingly good people worldwide are so hostile and inhumane to each other, and to know who Jesus is and what He really came for. If that is the result, then this book will have fulfilled my purpose in life in the light of Jesus of Nazareth, the living Son of the living Creator God.

To those who do not know they are walking in darkness by the way they think, act, speak, and live, and in their everyday treatment of their fellow humans, especially those they see as different or alien to themselves: may your eyes be opened to Jesus and the light and truth of His teachings in a dark world. This book is for everyone, regardless of your station in life. For those who think on a higher plane of understanding, the seekers of life's truths, this book is especially dedicated to you in the belief that it will convey to you the vastness of the Creator God and His wondrous creation, both on this earth and in the known and unknown universe. Remember, love is eternal. No act of love or kindness, no matter how small, is ever wasted in the kingdom of God. He will remember both you and your acts of love and kindness always. "Love one another," now and in the future.

Jesus, thank You for the truth You let me see in Your Word, the Bible, and for the revelation understanding Your Holy Spirit gives to all who will take time to listen. Thanks to all the ministers of Angel TV Channel and Christian Channel Europe.

Thanks to my grandma, Ena Josephine Humphreys, and my mother, Irene Hollywell, who prayed for me daily throughout my childhood, my teens, and later life, and to Barbara, who constantly prays for me and encourages me to seek God and have steadfast faith. These three showed boundless love and kindness to me and anyone God led to them – the poor, the down-and-outs, the people rejected by society, and anyone else who needed their help, rich, middle-class, or otherwise. They never turned any away. See you all in heaven – and on earth when Jesus returns with you all!

In the 1960's Gene Rodenberry created the series 'Star Trek' and used the following words. "Space, the final frontier. These are the voyages of Starship Enterprise. It's five year mission is to explore strange new worlds, to seek out new life and new civiklisations, to boldly go where no man has gone before." This is fiction! But there are spiritual realities into which people can be challenged to look. The full and real meaning of the Gospel about which I will be speaking is needed especially in Britain, but also in Europe.

In the beginning of the physical universe, suddenly in the darkness of infinite space and time, "There was light." How? *Seek* and you shall *find*. My name is John, but the name is not as important as the mind, soul, heart and spirit. As you read this book and *seek* to understand it, may the eyes of your spirit be opened, just as your physical eyes are open to colours and solid objects.

When we are born, a physical body comes out of our mother's womb. Inside that body, or shell, lives a spirit, the real person; inside that spirit lives a soul or mind. We are, in essence, a three-part being: body, mind, and spirit. This is the first birth. Yet in order to live forever, Jesus told us, our spirits must be born again or born a second time. Now! In this body! Not when we die, but now! The question is how?

Simple; *read on.*

There will always be the seekers. There will also be the sceptics and doubters until the end of time as we know it. *Seekers* want to know, really know where we came from, why we are here and where we go in the future and into *eternity*. However, there is coming a time, Jesus told us, when *all* people, male and female, will know the truth, not just in their minds but also in their spirits. There will be no sceptics in that time as everything will be clearly understood by all. That's *Good News*. Read 1Corinthians 13v12, 1John 2v2. The *bad news* is that not all men or women will enjoy this new-found knowledge. There are two places of existence, or consciousness, for our spirit after our bodies die. Most people know these places as heaven and hell. The truth is that heaven exists and hell is a real place, where real people will dwell for a long, long time. No one in their right mind will want to live in hell because they will be aware and conscious, still alive in hell, even though their physical body is dead.

Question: Is there a way for *all* people to avoid hell? The Good News is *yes*, and it's very simple: accept or ask Jesus of Nazareth to come and live in your heart. Simply believe and ask Him to come into your heart. He will come in, and your spirit will live forever with Jesus in the place called heaven. Suggested Bible readings are Romans 10:8-9, John 3:16, Revelation 22:14 In summary, speak out Jesus as Lord, with belief in your heart of His resurrection; understand that God loves you and offers you free access to the tree of life.

God knows you have many questions, and that's okay. Seek and you shall *find*. That's why this book has been written for you. Scientific questions will be answered; questions about evolution, spiritual questions, and questions about why there is so much poverty, suffering, and starvation on earth will also be answered. Many other questions will be answered too. Questions like "What is *faith* or *trust* in God?" will be answered in the most wonderful way. It's *Good News!* Will you now read on? The choice is yours. In Deuteronomy 30: 19–20, God said to Joshua and Israel (in paraphrase), "Choose this day life or death, blessing or curse." You choose too; the choice is *yours*.

Contrary to popular public belief and (sadly) church tradition, God is not sending people to hell. No, people choose heaven or hell! Surprised? It's the *truth*, and anyone who knows the truth of the Bible, which is the Word of God, will know hell is a prison, created to house the devil, Satan, and his demons, his fallen angels and evil spirits. Yet the devil, Satan, is fooling or deceiving people into choosing, unknowingly, the place of existence called hell. Read much more about Satan later in this book.

There is a Creator God, but there is also a fallen angel once called Lucifer, which means angel of light. We now call him Satan which, in English, means enemy of God or enemy of the people. God is the good guy, Satan is the bad guy, and both are real, live beings. They have a shape. They have arms, legs, head, etc. They are *real living beings* with a form. All spirits, including us, have a definite shape, and that shape is head, arms, body, legs, feet, hands, etc. Who is Satan or (*ha-satan*, which is Hebrew for "enemy")? His name was formerly the *nachash*, which means the shining one, and he was the anointed cherub. He's like an angel, with six wings, arms, legs, and head. He was an archangel, a ruler of angels.

In the book of Daniel (3: 24–25), Daniel's three friends are in the fiery furnace because they refused to worship the image of the king. They were not burned, but rescued by someone whom King Nebuchadnezzar recognised to be the Son of God; so Jesus was there thousands of years ago. Maybe some people will seek and through seeking find that *the answer is in Jesus of Nazareth, Messiah, God's Son,* and is found through His words and teachings.

In this book both God the Creator and I myself aim like an arrow to its target, to get your attention. So let's start now. Are you poor? No money or food, or struggling to pay debts? Read this book. There is a way out of your poverty. Money and food in abundance can be yours, and all your debts can be miraculously eradicated. Interested? Then read on. All the book must be read, though! Are you homeless, living on the streets or in squalor or even in a home or flat you would escape from now if you could? Good News. You can be provided with a new home of your dreams, but you will have to read the entire book to learn how to receive it.

Are you jobless, with no income or living on State benefits, and feeling hopeless? Read on. There is a job, a purpose, and a good income waiting for you – an answer, a practical answer, a way out. Are you sick or in poor health in body, mind, or spirit? Are you depressed or suicidal and would love to be healed, whole, and free of pain and torment? There is an answer. There is a way out, now, here on earth! Are you elderly and see no hope for your future? Are you fed up with daily hearing and reading people's lies and deceptions in the media and in person? Deep inside, do you really want to know the precise truth relating to your particular question or desire of your heart regarding any subject that's dear to you? Read on. This book, all of it, must be read and understood.

I'm calling all church denominations. Are you Protestant, Catholic, Methodist, evangelical, Pentecostal, Presbyterian, United Reformed, in fact any denomination? I'm calling all people. Are you white, black, brown, yellow, or red-skinned; short, tall, slim, medium, or large people? I'm calling all religious groups and sects – Muslim, Hindu, or even the non-believer. There is a treasure house of information and a blessing for you in this book. Interested? Then read on!

Who is God the Creator? What is He? Where did He originate? Where is He now? How do we contact Him? How can He contact us? Why are we here? Where did we come from? Where are we going? Questions,

questions! Yet there never seems to be an answer upon which everyone agrees. There always seem to be some points about God the Creator upon which people end up disagreeing

This book is intended for anyone who is seeking the answer, the one and only truthful answer about God and His purpose in creating mankind. I can almost hear you saying, "Oh no, not another book that claims to know *the truth* about God." I don't blame you for thinking this way, and neither does God. In fact, there have been so many untruthful "truth about God" books printed, people are entitled to say, "Enough of this rubbish, because it's all a mystery." No one can ever know the real truth about God and what He wants for human beings who live on this planet we call earth. They consult vicars, priests, pastors, church leaders, bishops, and popes, yet none of these people seem to agree totally.

It's possible, without putting a label on people, to ask you, the reader, which group of the following you fall into. Are you one of those who decide to get up and find out more about these questions? Or those who sit and wait for the answers? Maybe one of those who say, "We're too busy with day to day life to even give a thought to these questions"? How sad are the latter category, even though they probably don't realize it. Some may think after reading this that they have got it made. Anyway, without wasting their time seeking answers to what are to them such boring or unimportant questions, one of the aims of this book is to fire up the imagination of this third group.

Read on, as you will find interesting and stimulating subjects. What is faith? What does the word *faith* mean to you? What is the definition of faith? Do you have faith? If so, in what or in whom do you put your faith? Questions, questions. Is *faith* a word you feel is relevant in this materialistic, technological, and computer-oriented age?

Do you realize that you do actually have faith and unknowingly put it into practice each day? Think about it. Each day you wake up, get out of your bed, and flip the light switch. You have faith that the light will come on, and it does. You put your faith in the people who work at the electrical power station that the generators will work and that the flick of your switch will operate the light bulb. You do it without thinking; it's automatic, and you do it without understanding what electricity is. You do it without needing to see with your eyes the force called electricity. You believe it's there without seeing it. This is faith or trust.

CHAPTER 1

IN THE BEGINNING

The best place to start is always at the beginning, the origin. Suppose you were like the TV character Doctor Who, who travelled through space and time in his space-and-time machine, the Tardis. You could travel light-years in seconds, both forward and backward in time. If you arrived at a point, say, three thousand years ago in ancient Egypt, you could see exactly the way society worked, who the pharaoh was, and how the pyramids were built. You would know the answers from firsthand knowledge. Good news. Then when you got into your time machine and arrived back at our present time, you could look at books written by historians, scientists, archaeologists, or geologists and see any errors or truths in those books. You may be thinking, *If only we could do this, we would know precisely the truth of our planet's origin and of all its people.*

Obviously, there was a time when the earth did not exist, when the space now occupied by our large planet was empty. How did Earth and the stars and planets we see in the night sky get there? Most people want the answer. So upon what do the masses base these wonderful universes coming into being? Someone who was there when the first subatomic particle came into being? No! Upon whom, then? We can only trust Father God who was there when it all happened, but we cannot put 100 percent trust in human beings, no matter how educated they are. They are still fallible human beings. In order to know where humans, animals, plants, and insect life came from, we first have to know exactly where the earth came from. We have to know where our solar system came from, where our sun, an average-size yellow star, came from. We need to know exactly where our galaxy, a collection of approximately 100,000 million suns, came from. We need to know where all the space, seen and unseen, came from. We need to know exactly where the first single particle came from. To know this, we must know where the first basic components of the particle, an atom, came from. To identify where the first atom came from, we must know exactly where the first subatomic particles, which make up atoms, came from: electrons, protons, neutrons, neutrinos, photons (light particles), quarks, particles so small that one quark next to a single atom would be like a pinhead next to Mount Everest.

To know all these answers, someone would have to have been present back in time and at the exact location in infinite space to detect from where or from whom this first mind-boggling, tiny, solid particle came. Do we know of anyone, any human who can claim this? No. Even the most gifted scientific genius is guessing or theorizing about where our planet came from. Scientists would have to conclude that someone or some "being" with no beginning, no end, and infinite creative knowledge must be responsible for creating this first infinitesimal particle. This being with infinite power and intelligence we call God the Creator, a living, thinking being.

Yes, God exists. Read Romans 3: 4 and 16:25-27. God is true even when men try to judge Him wrong, as is proved by His power in peoples' lives manifested through the Scriptures, received by faith, by people all over the world. It's the only truly assessment possible. Why? Because even the first quark, photon, or atom must have come from something or someone. It is scientifically impossible for it to have just got here. Think hard; this is the only accurate, logical, and true explanation.

Question: Is there a book that records exactly this explanation of our origin, the earth, and the universe?

Answer: Yes, only one. We know it by the name of the Bible. It's the world's first and greatest accurate history book. To accept anything else – whether philosophy, models, or theories – is just guesswork and leads to confusion. Let's look at Genesis chapter 1, which says, "In the beginning, God created the heavens and the earth.." That's all known and unknown physical matter; there is a lot of this. Psalm 89: 11 says, "The heavens, (galaxies,) and earth belong to God. So scientifically and logically, the answer is that the Creator is the maker of all things, living and not living.

Therefore, it is to His Word, His revealed knowledge in the book we call the Holy (means perfect) Bible (made up of sixty-six small books), that we must look and to which we must compare all other knowledge. We will, in the end, put our faith and trust in either what God says or what humankind says.

Who was first, God or humans? Obviously, a creator is scientifically before the created; without a creator there is no creation. The Good News is that we are created, and God is our Creator. So the next question is Why did God create the heavens and the earth? Let's look for the answer. In the beginning was darkness, void; Genesis chapter 1 declares this. In Hebrew, *"Tohu whebo hu"*, translated as "without form and void" or "empty"

And God said (Gen. 1: 3), "Let there be light," and light was. Within this paragraph I am using the rendering of these verse from the original Hebrew.The very particles of light (photons) were created. Light travels at approximately 186,000 miles per second. With our knowledge of what light is and how it travels, it's easy to see the first chapter of Genesis as truth and fact, scientifically proven truth. Yet when the book of Genesis was written over three thousand years ago, people just had to believe there was a Creator God who spoke light into the void of space. Is the statement "Light be" (God said it and light appeared) any less true now than then? The answer is no. It was and is perfectly true. Today we understand more about light, making it easier for us to believe the accuracy of the statement, "Light be and light was.

Question: So how much more of the Bible that God said but we do not yet fully understand is true? All of it! We simply need to know and understand more of the truths revealed in the things God says. We need to do what Jesus said: "Seek and you shall find." Matthew 7: 7 says so. The Good News can be found in Jesus, the Son of God, who came from heaven to earth, and in His teachings, God's Word – God's promises to all humankind, His revealed truth and knowledge.

We are now at a point where you have to choose. Are you going to put your trust and faith in God, who is in Christ Jesus, and in what Jesus teaches in the sixty-six books of the Bible? Before you answer, let us take a good, intellectual look at exactly what faith and trust mean. Only when we understand what faith is can we use it. So what is faith exactly? The

Oxford English Dictionary describes faith as " Complete trust or confidence in someone or something.".

To conclude this chapter, I want all of you to know there is a way out for you from every heartbreak and every problem you face. Put your trust, your faith, in what Jesus said He will do for you. My prayer is that you will see the truth in all God has promised you, and you will receive all the manifestations of those promises. God really does love you personally. Please let Him into your life, into your mind, and into your spirit by simply asking for the Lord Jesus of Nazareth, the Messiah, God's Son, to come into your heart. Tell Him, "Lord Jesus, I believe you died for me, and I believe you rose and live again. Forgive me, and teach me all the rest of my life."

Say the above prayer aloud. You will never regret it. You will receive abundantly more now on earth than you ever imagined. You will also live forever with Jesus in paradise. Also when Jesus returns as king and brings you with Him, you will be with Him on planet earth.

The next chapter explains this in more detail. The choice is yours alone. Give Him the opportunity to teach you. Please read in your Bible Romans 10: 8–10 (key verse 10) and John 3: 16.

CHAPTER 2

FAITH AND THE
REASONS WHY

Research polls in America, Britain, and Europe show that the majority of people trust what their elite leadership say or teach. This elite numbers 10 per cent of the population. They are people of power who control how the others think, act, and live. That leaves the 1 per cent who actually know more, much more, and have much, much more in finances, goods, power, and influence than the majority of sheep and the 10 per cent of shepherds. These 1 per cent are the hidden influence behind the political and financial worlds. They are the multibillionaires and their specialist cadres of scientists, chemists, space technologists, genetic engineers, and others, including media, newspapers, TV, radio, education systems, and top universities. In essence, we have 1 per cent who *actually* know what they are doing and who exert great power, 10 per cent who *think* they know, and a large number who follow or trust the information given them by the elite leaders.

Question: Why is this dangerous?

Answer: Because without this knowledge, you will not know why you are in poverty and lack what you really need, why you are in ill health, and why you have to work long hours to earn just enough to live on. You may blame yourself, your parents, or just bad luck. The truth is that billions of people are starving to death, believing there is not enough money to buy them food. In reality, there is abundantly more than enough money to buy everyone on this planet the best food, a beautiful home, and fine clothes and to keep sickness down to a minimum. Most of us have been fed misinformation and have believed it. The consequence of this is death.

Question: What is the biggest cause of disease and sickness today?

Answer: Poverty (lack of money and material wealth).

Surprised? Read on! Insufficient money in Africa, India, Eastern Europe, etc., means people by the billions cannot afford medicines, simple operations, or hygiene products, nor do they have available to them clean drinking water, let alone sewers and sewage processing plants, resulting in disease due to living in filth. Ninety per cent of all deaths attributed to sickness and disease are due to lack of money.

Take heart; there is an answer, Good News for each of you, whether poor, sick, depressed, or powerless. Good News for you who have experienced pain, suffering, or defeat. Read on; the answers will be revealed through the promises that Jesus of Nazareth, the Son of the Creator God, gave to anyone who will put their trust and faith in Him and in what He said and promised.

Question: Haven't many people tried to change or reform the way things on earth are run? Change governments, change the inadequate health services worldwide, and bring in a new system, new ways of doing things that are fair and just?

Answer: Yes! From humanists to revolutionists, politicians to economists, philanthropists to rebel armies, countless people have "reformed" or partly changed one rotten system into another rotten system. The results are the same: injustice, lack, starvation, pain. So it would seem on the surface that things are pretty hopeless. That is exactly what the rulers of this world want you to think, and they always have. It is all lies. Yet people believe their lies because of a lack of knowledge of the truth, the exact truth. The 1 per cent of people who rule and control this planet are to blame.

Question: What do I consider enormous wealth, owned by one person or a small group of directors?

Answer: Enormous wealth is held by the owners of oil fields; owners of diamond, gold, silver, or precious metal mines; owners of gas fields, coal leases, or nuclear fissionable materials; owners of thousands of square miles of land and all the buildings and equipment on those lands; owners of lands producing huge quantities of coffee, tea, cotton, cocoa, etc.;

owners of enormous herds and flocks of livestock. An owner or group who own, for instance, a diamond mine in South Africa has in their control billions of pounds sterling daily flowing through their hands, banks, and strongboxes. Yet poverty and starvation are overwhelming. The money does not benefit the poverty-stricken people.

Question: Where does the money go which should be distributed to all in need?

Answer: Mainly to arms and weapons for armies worldwide. The vast amounts spent on space exploration programmes are enough to feed the world ten times over. Money to house and clothe the world ten times over is in vaults, banks, and underground strongholds like Fort Knox, doing nothing except satisfy the greed and ego of the super-rich, not to mention their small luxuries, such as yachts and top-of-the-range cars; they own numerous large mansions not lived in for most of the year. My point is that the wealth is there, but it's in the hands of a small minority, it's in the wrong hands and used for the wrong purposes.

Concerning this money – ongoing studies have shown that the richest 1 per cent of the world's population now owns more than 48 per cent of the global wealth. Of the world's wealth, 87 per cent is now in the hands of the top 10 per cent of people on earth. Ninety per cent of people own a mere 13 per cent of global wealth.

Between the years 2000 and 2008 inequality was decreasing, but since the financial crisis of 2008, inequality is now increasing again (documented by Thomas Picketty and reported in the Suisse Report of October 2014 and in the *Guardian* by Jill Treanor, 14 October 2014). Globally, household wealth has grown between 2013 and 2014 at the fastest rate ever recorded. However, the developing countries, e.g., China, with the highest population show that though they have 21 per cent of the world's adult population, they only have access to use 8.1 per cent of global wealth . Latin America has 8.4 per cent of the world's adult population but only 3.5 per cent of global wealth. In Africa and India the population exceeds wealth by a multiple of more than ten.

Question: What does God have to say about wealth?

Answer: In Haggai 2: 8 it says, "The silver is mine and the gold is mine, says the Lord Almighty." Psalm 50: 10 states, "I own the cattle on a thousand hills", whilst verse 12 says, "The earth is mine and the fullness thereof." Psalm 37: 11 states that the meek shall inherit the earth, and Jesus Himself said (Matt. 5: 5), "Blessed are the meek for they shall inherit the earth." In both these references the people being spoken of are those who are humble before God and know a dependence upon Him. In Proverbs 13: 22, the writer points out that the wealth of the sinner is laid up for the just. So a transfer of wealth is coming; we just need to know about it and lay hold by faith in what God says, in the same way that we learn to trust in God's promises for protection.

Money matters! Jesus said, through the apostle Paul "The love of money" is a root of all sorts of evil things (1 Tim. 6: 10).

Question: Why are we talking of money, and what has it got to do with God, Jesus and exact truth?

Answer: Many people have turned away from God because they were falsely told that He is not interested in them having money or material goods and that He said money is evil. This is a lie from Satan, the demons and the rulers of this world, yet 90 per cent of the world believes it. They have put their faith and trust in what others said about God without ever knowing the precise truth of what He really said. The truth is, God does want all people to have wealth, health, and a great education. In the Bible, where we may read what Jesus and His prophets and apostles from Old and New Testaments specifically said, anyone may find out for themselves. Are you interested? Then read on. It is Good News for you. You can now receive from God prosperity beyond your wildest dreams. Let's take a look at how to receive it and what God wants you to do with the wealth when you do receive it.

As with all things, we have to start at the beginning. The alphabet starts with the letter *A*, and the Bible starts with Genesis. Genesis is from a Hebrew word which translated into English means "the book of beginning". God is the author, starter, and creator of all things. We must find out what He has to say about money. His words, which are trustworthy, are written for us in the book that we call the bible. *Remember*, to see the whole finished jigsaw puzzle, every piece must be in its exact place. Likewise, this whole chapter and this whole book must be read by you, the reader.

Okay. Whoever you are – rich man, poor man, scientist, doctor, labourer, pilot, driver, banker, shop worker, housewife, husband, unemployed person, older man or woman – switch off for now the doubts, questions or fears in your mind and concentrate on what is written.

Jesus said in Revelation 1: 8, "I am the beginning and the end." Or as we read it, "I am the Alpha and the Omega." In Revelation 22: 12–14, He says, in my paraphrase, "I am the first and the last, blessed and empowered to prosper all those who wash their robes so that they [you] may have the right to [eat of] the Tree of Life and may go through the city gates into God's city."

Question: Who is empowered by God Himself to prosper and receive prosperity?

Answer: Jesus has promised in Romans 10: 8–11 that "if you believe in your heart and confess with your mouth the Lord Jesus and that God raised him from the dead, you shall be saved." This is the first step to receiving God's blessings of prosperity and receiving power from God so that you can prosper.

Jesus himself has *given* you the *right* to be blessed and prospered, to *live forever* and receive a resurrected body, the same type that Jesus received after three days and nights in the grave. You receive the right to live that life of prosperity forever in God's city as well as *now on earth.*

Question: If you want money, material things or wealth, why do you have to take the first step of asking Jesus, God's Son, into your life to be your Lord and Guide?

Answer: Here is the exact truth – it is all to do with a covenant, that is, an agreement or contract. When you receive Jesus into your heart and life, you enter into a contract or covenant with God –a contract by which God obligates Himself to do for you all that He promised (in the Bible) concerning all of the following things: He forgives you of all your wrongs; He gives you His eternal Spirit to live in you. This is Christ in you, living in you for a purpose. This person, the Holy Spirit, has power – power to carry out for you *all* that God has promised you in His Word (in the Bible), and it's signed by God in His blood, the blood of Jesus.

In order for you to fully receive *all* God has for you – money, peace, material goods, lands, health, and walking in love and goodness – you need to understand more about the covenant. As in any covenant or agreement between two people, each person agrees to do specific things for the other. Let's look at an earthly or human type of agreement, to give you some insight into a covenant relationship. Suppose you go to a shop to buy a television, and you agree to pay a certain amount weekly. The shop delivers the television to your house and agrees to repair or replace it free of charge if it stops working before the guarantee expires. By signing an agreement that states the terms and conditions, you both have a written copy of the contract or *covenant* to remind you (and also legal proof) of what you both promised. The contract is an *exact* written copy of what you both said or promised to do for each other.

The First Covenant Agreement

The first covenant on this earth was made about six thousand years ago between Adam and Eve and their Creator. In Genesis 1: 26 God said, "Let us make man in our image and in our likeness." Adam and Eve knew exactly who was making a covenant or agreement with them, and they also knew that they were the created children of God. They knew about covenant, to put it simply in English, because God said, "If you break agreement by eating of the tree of the knowledge of good and evil, the consequence is death." Adam and Eve knew.

Eve was not created until after Adam was instructed not to eat of this tree. Adam got his instruction straight from God, but not Eve. Her understanding of it came from Adam. Hence she added the part about "neither shall you touch it". This was an agreement between the parent and the children, a family agreement.

Question: What was Adam and Eve's part in the covenant, which they freely and with understanding entered into?

Answer: God put Adam and Eve into a garden called Eden and told them, "You can eat of all the fruit from any tree in the garden except for one thing only. In the middle of the garden, next to the tree of life with its fruit, is a tree of the knowledge of good and evil. All I ask of you is that you do not eat any fruit from this one tree. If you do, you will die." That was Adam and Eve's part. That's all! Sadly, Adam and Eve did eat of the fruit of the tree of the knowledge of good and evil; they broke their part of the covenant. Just as God said, Adam and Eve both died, having passed on the knowledge of evil to all their children. Their children passed on the knowledge of evil to their children and descendants, right up to the present time.

Question: What was God's part in the covenant or agreement with Adam and Eve?

Answer: Read Genesis 1: 27–29 in your Bible. God blessed them and said to them, "*Be fruitful, increase* in number, and fill the earth. *Subdue* it, *rule* over fish, birds, and all living creatures that live on the ground." Let's break it up into individual parts to understand the agreement of what God said He would do for Adam (mankind) if they did the one thing He asked them to do.

Number 1

God gave them power to get wealth, to get health, to get material goods, to get peace, and to be happy, power to have knowledge and wisdom, and power to act in love. The Hebrew word *shalom* is exclusively used to describe a state of completeness and wholeness, with nothing missing in any area. That was how Adam and Eve were originally, whole and complete. The exact truth is that *shalom* means having nothing missing from any area of your life, nothing broken, but rather having completeness and wholeness. Adam and Eve were eternal beings. How do we know Adam and Eve were eternal creatures with God's power on and in them? Easy, God made them in His image. God is clothed outside and inside with limitless power to be and to do anything good that He wants to.

Number 2

Be fruitful. God gave them power to increase in every area of life: to increase in good and charitable works, in learning and knowledge, and in love for God and each other; to be fruitful towards all humankind and animal kind. Adam and Eve were in a perfect state before they ate; they knew only good, and they were empowered to be good and charitable towards each other. They would have been absolutely perfect. "Multiply" speaks for itself: they were to produce others like themselves who were perfect. Fill the earth with people in God's likeness. They looked like God, and their image, character and heart were like God's.

Number 3

By "subdue", God meant they were to take control of the earth and the creatures in it, not let the creation control them. Genesis 1: 28 implies it was to be done with love. A"B'rdam and Eve were made perfectly in God's image, unlike present-day humans. When God blessed them and said, "Be fruitful … have dominion", this meant rule with power. As God is love, Adam and Eve could only do this with love.

Number 4

They were to rule – that is, have power, control and rules, good rules, and apply these good rules to the earth, its creatures, and everything in it. God is a God of order, who has rules and laws, e.g., the law of gravity. He also has the "love rule": Without good, loving rulership over the animals and creatures of the earth, Adam and Eve would have mistreated and killed Earth's creatures, as we see today.

Number 5

Every seed-bearing plant and every tree with fruit has seeds in it. God gave them the fruit of the trees and plants and the seeds in them so they could eat the fruit and sow the seeds. More fruitful trees and plants would be grown for food.

Number 6

God gave every green plant for food to all creatures of the earth that walked, crawled, swam or flew. In the beginning God did not give the meat of animals to humans for food. Nor did He give to animals other animals to eat. Nothing was meant to die. Everything was originally created to live in peace together forever. Don't worry, I'm not saying you can't eat meat; eat it if you want to. The point is, it is not God's best for humankind or animal kind.

Due to Adam's choosing the knowledge of evil, death came into the world. This was the first sin. To sin means to break a perfect command or law, either by choice or through ignorance, not knowing right from wrong. Adam knew his actions were wrong. He chose to know evil. Today we see evil worldwide. Death and the evils connected to it are now in this world through the breaking of the first covenant. Sadly, Adam and Eve have passed on their knowledge of evil to all mankind, and a further effect is that we now have Adam's nature and physical D.N.A.

Adam did have some help. He was tempted when presented with bait as when a fisherman puts a worm or maggot on his fish hook. The fish sees the tasty bait and chomps on it. *Lovely*, thinks the fish, but suddenly the hook, hidden by the bait, is firmly caught in the fish's mouth, and the fish is now in the fisherman's hand, ready to go into the frying pan.

Read Genesis 3: 1–4, where you will see that the evil fisherman in the garden of Eden was Satan (now read Ezekiel 28: 13–14). The Hebrew word *ha-satan* means simply "enemy" (Satan). He is a rebel angel from heaven, a cherub-type angel whose name was Lucifer, which means "angel of light". The Bible says he was the anointed angel, but he rebelled against God's commands, God's way of doing things.

Lucifer wanted to be the king of the universe and all creation. Lucifer said, "I will be like the Most High God and take His place." God kicked him and all the other rebel angels out of heaven, one third of the total number of angels. Jesus said in Luke 10: 17–20, "I saw Satan fall like lightning from heaven to the earth." This was the first alien invasion. A species called angels, bad ones, now called demons, are thus on earth, and their first dastardly, dirty deed was to deceive Adam and Eve in the garden of Eden.

Bah! Worm delicacy, worm on the line! Adam bit and got hooked, and he and all his descendants died. Adam chose Satan and his ways instead of God and His ways. Today we have the same choice: either Jesus and His ways or Satan with his demons and their ways. Which will you choose? What you choose will lead to blessings and prosperity on earth and eternally in the world to come if you make Jesus the Lord and Master of your life (John 3: 16 explains). Alternatively, you can choose Satan and his ways, which leads to curses and death on earth.

Read the 28th chapter of Deuteronomy, verses 15-68. these verses are known as the curse of the law of the old covenant, which God made with

Moses and the Jews; those who were the physical descendants of Abraham. Read it please. The curses were sickness, poverty, depression, failure, fear, lack, lack of success, broken marriages, and death. Then when your spirit leaves your body after your flesh dies, your spirit and mind go to a prison (hell) with Satan. God is sending no one to hell. People are choosing to go there – that is, once they know the truth of God's Word.

You must recognize that there are two judgements; if you have heard and refuse to make Jesus Lord and Saviour, when you die, you will ultimately go into the lake of fire. This is the second death and is because your name is not written in the Lamb's book of life. The only way to get your name in there is by accepting Jesus as Lord and Saviour.

Then there are people who have never heard the gospel and they will be judged differently –with mercy and justice, because if they have never heard the gospel, how can they ask Jesus into their life? So as the Word tells us in Romans 10: 8–10, "if anyone will believe in their heart and confess with their mouth that Jesus is their Lord and that He died for them and that God raised Him from the dead, he (or she) shall be saved" – from hell, Satan, and the curses of the law.

Romans goes on (verses 11–15) to say, "How can they believe (the truth) unless someone tells them (the truth, God's Word)? How can they choose unless they have been educated to the truth?" That's my job, to tell you the truth. *The answer is Jesus Christ the Saviour.* Please, ask Jesus into your heart.

You just learned about the first covenant between God and Adam (first mankind, male and female), which was broken, leading to death, evil on earth and later hell (the prison of spirits). That's bad news. Read 1 Peter 3: 18–21 for more insight.

But the Good News Is for Anyone

Whoever you are, if you will accept Jesus as your Lord God or Master, God has promised He will make a new agreement with you, a new and better covenant. Please read John 3: 16. In order to understand this agreement better, we will now briefly look at the exact meaning of the word covenant as it translates the Hebrew "b'rit". It means "a binding agreement between two parties or people".

Readers, you must understand that when God makes a covenant He cannot break it. It says this in Psalm 89:34. "My covenant I will not break nor alter the word that has gone forth out of my mouth". These are the promises that God has said He will do for us who are believers in Jesus who are heirs to the blessing. Galatians 3:29 and3:13-14 explains this. God seals His covenants in blood, in our case, the blood of the Lamb Jesus. He will always do what He said He will do. He will always act on His part of the bargain, if you do your part. So take note: once you study God's Word, accept only what is written. Do not allow anyone to attempt to misinterpret what God has specifically said. Beware, there are many well-meaning people around to help you disbelieve what Jesus promised, even Christians, vicars, theologians, bishops, archbishops, and popes as well as nonbelievers, scientists, philosophers, intellectuals, Jehovah's Witnesses, Mormons, etc., because of their lack of knowledge of the exact truth and revelation of what God has said exactly in his Word, the Bible.

Read Hosea 4: 6. It's important. It says,"My people (believers) perish, are destroyed, through a lack of knowledge of my word." So from God's own mouth, clearly revealed, is the reason why God's own people perish or are destroyed. Please, don't you be one of them. Diligently and slowly, study God's promises and instructions each day, do what they tell you to do, and believe what God said He will do for you. Is one hour a day too much? We (most of us) watch TV for four or five hours a day, so come on, wise up. Don't perish through a lack of knowledge of the covenant agreement.

Then, if anyone, even a church leader, says God won't do this or that or God did not mean this or that or He meant something else, you will know right away what's true and what's false. The alarm bells will go off in your heart or spirit; you will learn like an old bull or cow, eat the straw and spit out the sticks, the lies and misinterpretations. Please now read slowly, take it in: this is how God has always made a covenant since the fall of Adam. God always seals His promises in blood. You are shocked? Well, it's true.

In order to receive all God has for you personally, wonderful things, you must first understand exactly how God's blood covenant works. Once

15

we understand the first blood covenant between God and Abraham, we can then understand the second blood covenant between God and Abraham's seed, Jesus; the promises God made us for today through the blood of Jesus in the New Testament.

Abraham – in English it means "father of many nations" or "great multitudes of children" – and God made (in Hebrew) a *b'rit*. In English this means "a bond or fetter", indicating a binding loyal relationship based on *chesed* (love). This is the loyalty and friendship type of covenant that King David and Jonathan, Saul's son, had. This *chesed* (pronounced "hesed") love mixed with the *b'rit* blood was irrevocable. No going back on the agreement – this is the one God made with Abraham – and the promises of total prosperity were to Abraham and his descendants and to a person called Abraham's seed. According to Scripture, God's Word, this man's name was Messiah. The Hebrew word *mashiach* translated into English, means "the anointed one" or "God's anointed king", and God made to Abraham many great promises. God promised that anyone (and their family) descended from Abraham and his Seed, the Messiah, would receive all things promised to Abraham.

A *b'rit* worked in Israel thousands of years ago as follows: There were many rebel armies and brigand-bandit gangs and cruel nations with marauding armies who would loot, rape, and pillage, slaughter the men, and take the women and children as slaves and all that they owned as loot or booty. So to avoid all these disasters, a group of shepherds who owned livestock but were weak or under- armed would make a covenant or *b'rit* with the local tribal army, and they would each promise to share their strengths and goods. So now the army had all they needed, and the shepherds had protection.

In the presence of the local leaders, elders, kings, and generals, they would each swear an oath and say what they would do. Then they would have scribes write it on stone tablets or on scrolls, and each would be given a copy in writing of exactly what each side had sworn on oath to do. Finally they would set a time limit, a minimum of eight or even ten generations, which spanned 300 to 400 years or more, so that even the children of the shepherds and the children of the army kept the same agreement after the death of the fathers and mothers who had originally made the agreement.

To make it totally binding, it was sealed in a blood rite using the very best animal. The slain animal, either a lamb or a bull, would be cut in half, then a representative from each party would walk between the two halves of the animal, walking over the blood. They would be doing this whilst exchanging vows, weapons,goods and coats. They then cut the palms of their hands and clasped hands together, thus mixing blood before finally sharing a meal and mixing family names.

All this was done with God as witness, that if any of them broke their promises, they would be put to death, and God would ensure the penalty was paid for any treachery or breaking of a promise. So even if there were only 500 farm boys and shepherds being attacked by an army of ten thousand, the covenant partners, the local army, even if they only had four thousand troops, would fight the ten thousand invaders to the death. That is total loyalty; their word was their bond for as long for as the contract was established. What reassurance and peace of mind that brought to both parties.

Chesed, in English, is a cut where blood flows. Now blood is the life-carrying liquid which the human body and brain need to exist. Take away that blood, drain it off, and no matter how fit or healthy you are, you will die. So there is no more precious possession that a man, a woman, or God could give as a surety or guarantee that they both would keep their promise to one another than the life force of their bodies, that is, their blood. That's why God, yes, God introduced blood covenants after Adam (the first man) broke his covenant with God in Eden. God killed an animal, shed its blood, and used its skin and fur to clothe Adam and Eve (Gen. 3: 21). Read also Genesis 18: 17–19 where Abraham declares that the covenant God made with him stated that God said, "I know him, he will teach his children of My ways, right and wrong, and the covenant, so that I may keep My promise to him and his descendants."

Question: Why did God want Abraham to teach his family and descendants?

Answer: So that no one would ever forget their covenant rights with God and that all his descendants would pass on their knowledge of the covenant from generation to generation forever. That is why the Lord has inspired me to write this book, to make everyone who reads it aware of the original and exact covenant promises made to you who have Jesus as Lord and Saviour.

Do you understand it? It was God's blood that was shed on the cross. Jesus said to his disciples at the Passover meal (the Last Supper), "Take this cup of wine, this is my blood of the new covenant shed for you and for many for the forgiveness of sins" (see Matt. 26: 27–28). Before Jesus came to earth, people's sins could be forgiven only according to the Abrahamic covenant, by the shedding of blood. So instead of God having to kill Abraham or his descendants, which the covenant agreement demanded, God said, "If you do wrong, kill a lamb or a calf or a ram. Shed its blood (the scapegoat's) instead of yours." Horrible, but it was better than humankind having to pay the price, until God could get Himself onto this planet in a body, so He could, once and for all, shed His blood and make an everlasting covenant with all humanity.

He stated that all who would accept Jesus and His sacrifice of blood on the tree or cross would be forgiven of all wrongdoing, be given eternal life, and have God's own Spirit live inside them. Jesus died In our place: this is the great exchange; on the Cross Jesus took our curse , sickness, sorrows, poverty and sin so that now we can have what He gave us, forgiveness, righteousness, right standing with God, health, wealth, wholeness and all the blessings of the Abrahamic covenant. In Hebrew this means the empowerment to prosper in all areas of life. Jesus died in our place so that we would not have to pay the price for our wrongs and so that our spirits would not have to go to hell, the prison for everyone rebelling against God and His loving instructions. He gave His Spirit to live inside anyone who will accept Jesus, to impart a new birth to our old spirits, so we could be born again in God's image and likeness and have our minds renewed to line up with the requirements of the covenant so that we may receive all His promises. Read John 3 (you must be born again). Without Jesus and His Spirit living in us, this is impossible.

Wherever you are, ask Jesus *now:* "Come into my heart and fill me; baptize me with Your Holy Spirit now, Lord. I receive You." He will come into your life immediately, wherever you are. Trust Him to do it, and just know He's *in* you. Why? Read Revelation 3: 20, "Here I am. Behold, see I stand at the door knocking, if anyone hears my voice and opens the door, I will come (in) and eat with them." Ephesians 6: 11 tells Christians (anointed ones who follow Jesus, who have asked Jesus into their lives), to put on the whole armour of God. We have a blood covenant, the blood of the Lamb, Jesus. We now share all God's possessions and strengths. We can wear God's coat, replacing failure, wrongdoing, poverty, depression, sickness, weakness, and death, with all the authority and power His garment represents. God is our Father; we are His family. It doesn't matter who is wearing the armour or coat of God; it's the coat or armour which does the talking and carries the authority and benefits.

Praise Jesus, who gave His blood in our place so anyone who accepts Him as Lord comes into an eternal blood covenant relationship with God, and all He has is yours! No more sacrifices are required by God. Jesus paid the price by becoming the sacrificial lamb for all who will accept Him and confess Him as Saviour. In Matthew 18: 19–20, Jesus said, "If any two of my followers agree on earth, concerning any need, desire, or want and shall ask of God in My name, it shall be done for them by My Father God, who is in heaven. For where two or three are gathered together in My name, there will I be also (to carry out the agreement) in the midst of them."

Most of the church has never fully understood this. What it means, exactly, is that the covenant agreement is based on the blood of Jesus and the scars on his hands and feet where the nails of the cross were fixed. What Jesus says, He means: "Any two who are in Jesus Christ, asking anything of God and agreeing, not doubting, it shall be done." It will be done on earth now – a house, a car, food, clothes, furniture, etc. It's true. You have Jesus' word and blood! Believe it, receive it, do it; it works! God must do it for you because if you are in Christ, He has sworn by His blood to give any two who agree what they have asked God for.

Ephesians 3: 15 says the whole family of Jesus is named of God the Father, in heaven and earth. Jesus is the name that is above every name and more powerful, carrying more authority, than any other name on earth or in the spatial heavens and God's heaven. Mark 16: 15–18 says, "Go into all the world and baptize all the nations into My name and those who believe on My name shall be saved and not condemned (by God's judgement). And in My name they will lay hands on the sick and they shall recover, they shall cast out (Satan) the enemy and his demons (fallen angels), in My name, speak in new tongues (languages), and in My name no deadly poison shall harm them." See, when God's people use the name of Jesus, all things obey. It's just the same as if Jesus Himself were personally present and personally laying hands on the sick and releasing power to miraculously heal them.

See the covenant swap? God's power in exchange for your lack and weakness. You have His Word and His blood to confirm it, as total, precise truth. This is Good News! So now, in truth, you are a family member named of Jesus, and anything you ask that's good in Jesus' name shall be given to you as long as you are keeping your part of the covenant. We can still make our own choices and "do our own thing" if we so desire. But remember, whatever God has promised in His Word – and there are over seven thousand promises that are good and relate to eternal life, forgiveness, financial prosperity, long life, divine health, and the protection of angels – is available to us. That is the purpose of this book – to teach what is God's will. Ours is a covenant between a resurrected (from death) immortal Man named Jesus and a Holy (perfect) infallible God (the Father). Which of them do you think could ever break the covenant?

Answer: Neither of them, ever. The Good News is, neither can we break it. Yes, it's true, when you belong to Jesus, you cannot break the covenant.

Question: Why not?

Answer: We have been grafted into a covenant. As Jesus died on the cross, He said, "Oh Lord, Father, be merciful, forgive them; they do not know what they are doing." God raised Jesus from the dead to life everlasting, and He has been showing mercy to the family of Jesus ever since and always will. God always answers Jesus' prayers. When you ask for anything using Jesus' name, God is all ears! He still remembers the words, "Father, forgive them."

But you will have to let go of all your old traditions and religious ideas, taught you erroneously by people who themselves have been deceived by Satan, through the media, other church leaders, and so-called "learned teachers". What will you choose to do now? Learn more about what God said is yours or about what deceived humankind says is not yours? Are you listening? I pray you will! Have you heard lies? – for example, that God puts poverty on people, that the Lord God gives and takes away, or puts or allows sickness to come on people to test them or teach them a lesson? Lies, all lies! The Word of God does not say any of this! Seek and you shall find.

Simply get your copy of the blood covenant out and remind yourself and God of what He said, what He promised on oath to you. This is *faith* in God's ability and faithfulness to do for you what He said. If or when the devil (yes, it's him who brings diseases, sickness, poverty, oppression, fear, worry, harm, threats, etc.) comes against you, remember the covenant! Remember the blood. Now, at last, there is a way out and an *answer* for your particular problem.

Don't wait any longer. Make Jesus your Lord today.

CHAPTER 3

CAUSE AND EFFECT

Before we receive anything from God through Jesus and His promises, we must first of all realize that we have an enemy, Satan and his fallen angels. Their two main weapons are deception and confusion. The devil knows that if he can get you to speak aloud your negative and fear-filled thoughts, he can bring them into reality. Jeremiah 1: 12 says that God watches over His word, His promises, to perform them. Psalm 103: 20–21 says that all God's angels hearken (keep their eyes and ears open), ready to carry out God's words.

Question: What are your weapons against the devil?

Answer: Many, if you have Jesus in your life.

Jesus says, in Mark 16v17-18 " And these signs shall follow them that believe; in my name shall they cast out devils; they shall speak with new tongues. They shall take up serpents and if they drink any deadly thing it shall not hurt them; they shall lay hands on the sick and they shall recover." Luke 10v19 says, " Behold I give unto you power to tread on serpents and scorpions, and over all the power of the enemy; and nothing shall by any means hurt you." The words used in the Greek are dunamis and exousia, which mean power and authority. The first thing to understand is that financial prosperity and health are intertwined. Money buys food, clothes, medicines, and housing. Because people lack money to buy food, they starve; they lack money to buy clothes so they freeze; they lack money to buy homes, so they are homeless or live in terrible shacks with no sanitation. They lack money to buy medicines or hospital care for diseases and sickness caused by their filthy, unhygienic flea pits.

Would you want money for medicine, toilets, food, clothes, and sanitary and hygienic conditions, the simple basics of human (bodily) existence? Yes! We will deal with God and money and His desire for you to have it and use it correctly in the next chapter. First, let me speak to you all about how to avoid disease and get crippling sickness off your bodies, even stunted or damaged limbs replaced, now, today in this life on earth! First, you must know your enemy. The Spirit of Jesus said in Ephesians 6: 12, "we do not wrestle (or fight) against flesh and blood (people) but we do fight against powers, against rulers of the darkness (the evil) of this world and against spiritual wickedness (wicked evil spirits) in high places." There are fallen angels who rule in the 2nd heavens, a dimension where fallen angels dwell. This is just below the 3rd heavens where God and His angels rule and dwell.. One of Satan's oppressions is sickness. Read and digest the following verses. Acts 10: 36–38: The Holy Spirit of God said through the apostle Peter, "You know the message of God sent to all Israel's people, how God anointed Jesus of Nazareth with the Holy Spirit and with power, who went about doing good and healing all that were oppressed of the devil, for God was with Him." This passage says that all oppression is from the devil. All sickness is oppression from the devil. Jesus only went about doing good and healing all who were oppressed of the devil, and He did it with the power of God, who was with Him and who had anointed Him with the Holy Spirit and power. So, all sickness is oppression! Yes, and all sickness is from the devil.

You must know exactly, without doubt, that Satan is your enemy and that this enemy uses sickness as a weapon to oppress you. Other weapons are fear, poverty, and lack of knowledge. You must know that your friend and God is Jesus, who always goes about doing good and healing all whom the devil oppresses with sickness and disease of all kinds. You must know that *you* have the power and release it in the name of Jesus.

Now, read Luke 13: 10–16. On a Sabbath (the Jewish holy day held on the seventh day of the Jewish week, which in English we call Saturday), Jesus was teaching in one of the synagogues (buildings where Jews met to hear their Scriptures, the Old Testament, being read and taught by the Jewish rabbis). A woman was there who had been crippled by a spirit (demon devil spirit) for eighteen years. She was bent over and could not straighten up at all. The key verse is 11; it's not a disease but an evil spirit. In verse12 we are told that "when Jesus saw her He called her forward and said to her, 'Woman, you are set free from your infirmity'" Then in verse 13, "He put (laid) His hands on her, and immediately she straightened up, and she praised God." In verse 14 we are told that that the ruling rabbi of the synagogue bemoaned and criticized Jesus. Jesus called him a hypocrite for his lack of love and mercy. See Satan at work on the rabbi? So, in verse 16, a key verse, Jesus said, "Should not this woman, a daughter of Abraham, whom Satan has kept bound for eighteen years now, be set free on the sabbath day?"

Here we must note the following things. Jesus said the woman was a daughter of Abraham, and she had in covenant the right to be set free from the crippling spirit. Most important, it seems that this woman did not know that, because she was Abraham's seed, she had access to all the promises of Abraham provided by the blood covenant cut between God and Abraham – that she had a right to be healthy and free. It was Jesus who spoke and revealed this truth to the woman in verse 16. Today, God's Spirit still reveals it to you! Praise God.

Now get this, in Hosea 4: 6, God said, "My people (his own believers) are perishing (being destroyed) because of lack of knowledge, for you have forgotten (or you don't know) the word of God (the commands and promises)."

Question: Why are people suffering on earth? Followers of Jesus and those who are not God's people are perishing through early death, disease, lack, poverty, depression, broken relationships, etc.

Answer: They lack knowledge of the real cause of all their problems, the existence of a fallen angel and his evil followers, demons, who are responsible for most of the trouble and horrors in this world. They lack knowledge of the power, the authority, over these fallen angels or demons and evil that they have (if they are in Christ Jesus) or that they could have if they asked Jesus into their life (so ask Him in *now*). They lack knowledge of exactly what God has said and how they should understand precisely what He says and promises and means. Sadly, for the most part, many lack the knowledge that the book we call the Bible is a written copy of what God has said, promised, and sealed in the blood (covenant) of Jesus.

For instance, if there was an invisible and silent murderer on the loose, who walked up to anyone he chose and shot them with an unseen gun, and all the evidence left at the murder scene was a dead body, how many different explanations would people come up with over, say, a thousand-year period? There are two things that would accompany these deaths. Panic – fear that you would never know the day it could happen to you – and sadly, acceptance that at some time in your life, death would visit you. As a result, you wouldn't even try to fight the inevitable certainty that one day you, too, would just drop dead from this unknown enemy.

This is exactly what is happening on earth today. It's similar to what the Bible calls "types and shadows". The enemy is unseen, unheard, or so people think, and his weapons are deadly and silent. Disease and poverty, leading to early death in millions of people worldwide. People are perishing through a lack of knowledge of exactly where and whom disease comes from and how to stop it. Satan is highly intelligent and has great knowledge of this earth and how things work, including chemistry, science, medicine, biological warfare, etc. However, Satan is stupid for becoming God's enemy. Only a fool, no matter how powerful or intelligent, would attack the Creator of the universe, his own creator. Lucifer, who became Satan, is a created being. God was never created! He has always existed; that's why He is God (in a body named Jesus).

If you don't know from where and from whom troubles come, you will be miserable and have the most precious things in life stolen from you and be destroyed, all because of your lack of knowledge of the root cause. This often results in God being blamed. Many preachers, ministers, and vicars make this mistake by saying, "The Lord gives and the Lord takes away. God is responsible for every action on earth, good or bad, births and deaths, health and disease, riches and poverty, the exact opposites, bad and good." No! The Bible clearly says this is a lie from Satan. All evil is from Satan working through people who decide there is no God, no devil, and we just appeared here and evolved. Satan also works through people who say that they believe there is a God but don't have a relationship with Him.

Then there are people who don't even think about God; they are just going through the motions of their life, and if people get hurt, "Not my problem!" They don't want to believe in or follow a God who brings or allows such random suffering on this earth. Who in their right mind can blame them? God does not. That's why God sent Jesus to tell people the truth. The truth is that God is good, and He is Love. His will is His Word, His Word is His will.

So if you really want to know what God's will is for you, then read the Bible daily, and you will find out exactly what God's will really is for you (all) personally concerning lack, poverty, sickness, and the rest.. The truth is, you will find the devil is evil. His will is to bring disaster on humankind and to wipe them out (if he could), and his weapons are very evil: sickness, poverty, depression, suicide, war. He uses people to manifest the evils.

Let's look at some of the religious and traditional errors and false beliefs about God. It's essential for you to learn how to recognize the difference between what God has said exactly to you in the covenant and what it seems that God said. The difference is not only truth or error but life or death, health or sickness, success or very painful failure or even accepting the loss of a beloved child, wife, or husband at a young age. Be on your guard: a well-meaning, God-loving person or religious leader may tell you that something bad or unwanted in your life is from God, when in truth it is not. Although it can sound plausible, don't accept or buy the lies. Don't be angry with them because they are perishing through a lack of knowledge of what God has really said, and they are passing on this error to countless others; it's tragic.

The central character of Revelation 12: 7–17 is the serpent who deceives the nations. The mastermind behind their teaching, traditions, errors, deceptions, is the devil. Read this verse to see how he does it and how he got here in the first place. After he and his angel followers decided they would no longer obey God and His commands, and Lucifer decided he would depose God and sit on His throne and rule the universe instead of God. Revelation 12: 7–9 says, "Then war broke out in heaven." Archangel Michael and his angels, two-thirds of the total number of the heavenly host, waged war upon the dragon (Satan, formerly named Lucifer). The dragon (Satan) and his angels fought against God's angels, but they did not have the strength or power to win, and no foothold was left for them in heaven. So that great dragon (Lucifer), along with his angels (demons), was thrown down, that serpent of old who led astray the whole world (people of earth), whose name is Satan (enemy). This explains that he and his angels were defeated in war and fled here. Because they are spirit beings, they have the ability to be either invisible or visible to human eyes. They are mainly invisible as that's the way they prefer it to be, so you don't know you have an enemy. It's similar to earthly , guerrilla warfare, where enemies are in your midst, unknown and ready to strike at random times.

Question: How can we know Satan is here now? How can we know without seeing with our physical eyes that Satan and his demons are here now and that they are the unseen enemy bringing evils of all types on mankind?

Answer: We trust God's Word, what He said in the Bible. It's the only way to know exactly who the enemy is, what he is here for, where he came from, what his nature is (evil), and what his weapons are. Once we know this, the fear of him and his weapons and the mystery of why bad things are happening in this world are clear to us. Let's look at some revealing Scriptures, which will help us see exactly where the fallen angels (these rebels) came from, why they are here, where they are destined to go, and what are our weapons, right now, to destroy their works on earth and in our lives. The Good News is in Jesus. Our weapons are mighty, much stronger than Satan's. Read Ephesians 6: 10–18 and 2 Corinthians 10: 4.

We have read from God's Word that Satan came from God's dwelling place, heaven, and he is here because he lost his battle with God and His angels. There is no place for him in heaven. He is on earth now because when he was thrown out of heaven; this is the planet he fled to, where God had made humanity in His image. Satan decided that if he could not take God's home and rule, he would settle on humankind's home planet and rule. This power he succeeded in obtaining by deceiving the woman called Eve in the garden of Eden. Adam willingly watched and ate of the tree of knowledge of good and evil, thereby agreeing to have Satan rule over him as his new leader or Lord. The word we translate from the Hebrew as "Lord" means "master".

Satan's aim was now to infect and infiltrate humanity so that he could legally keep planet Earth. Adam had handed his authority over the earth to Satan. So Satan had a legal right to be here, even though he had used deception to get it. This is why God had to send Jesus, to win back humanity and planet Earth before Satan could destroy us and have a safe haven for himself and the demons forever.

But thanks be to God, to Jesus! Jesus won back planet Earth two thousand years ago. Good News. He has provided a way for all people to have eternal life in Christ Jesus and a way for us to have everything promised in the Word, the Bible, through His blood, making us partakers of all the promises of Abraham given to Jesus and anyone who has or will make Jesus their master. (All except the land of Israel, that is, which was given to Abraham and his Jewish descendants.)

Faith works by love. Hell is a prison made for the devil and his angels. Matthew 25: 41 tells us that Jesus said to those who had refused to believe in him and ask him into their life, "Depart from Me (go away), you who are cursed (under the curse of the law; see Deut. 28: 15–68), into the eternal fire prepared for the devil and his angels." So you can see that the prison, hell, was only created for the devil and his angels, but people can still choose to go there by simply not accepting Jesus as their Lord, Master, and Saviour. Hell was not created for mankind! God wants no one to go to hell. No! John 3: 16 says so: "God loves all in the world and wants no one to perish; He sent His only Son, Jesus, so that whosoever believes in Him (Jesus) shall not perish but have eternal life!"

Yet you, like Adam and Eve, still have free will, the right to choose Jesus and eternal life or say no with the penalty of spending (and that's not maybe) eternity in hell with Satan. So, today, simply choose Jesus! It's easy! I urge you, please, please accept God's way out now, and also receive all the blessings of the blood covenant here on earth, plus eternal life in heaven. Later on you will be in the new earth with God forever, and you also get a new, immortal flesh body that will never die but stay young forever. You will never have to grow old or ever get sick again, once resurrected.

Choose now, because even though the devil is a defeated enemy he is still here on earth for a short time and he can still attack you unless you use the weapons given by the Holy Spirit, which God gives to all who receive Jesus as Lord. However, you must know how to use them. Let's look now at what the devil's limited arsenal is and what our unlimited, super powerful weapons are.

The devil's weapons first, because they are few

He uses confusion and deception. Revelation 12: 9 informs us that "he deceives the people in the world." Think about it. If you don't know the truth about a particular subject or thing or person, how would you know who was telling you the exact truth about the subject or thing? You wouldn't know. Read in your Bible 2 Corinthians 4: 4, which says, "the god of this world, this age (, has blinded (confused) the minds of the unbelievers (who have not known God or Jesus, His living Word) so they cannot see the light of the Gospel (the teachings and Good News) of the glory, power, and truth of Christ Jesus, the Anointed One." Here Paul says that the god of this world is Satan, who blinds and confuses the minds of people against the exact truth, to stop the Gospel or Good News taught by Jesus from being understood, accepted as the truth, and believed or trusted in. The truth is that God intended that everyone should understand the Gospel.

Satan is not God, but the Greek word that the translators have rendered as "god of this world" means "ruler of the minds of the unbelievers in this world". He's a god over them. He's not God but a ruler or lord over certain people's thoughts, ideas, and understanding. He confuses and deceives people's minds and thoughts so that they don't know or recognize the truth. We have God's Word, and God Almighty, El Shaddai, the God who is more than enough, has had it written down for us so we can read it anytime, anywhere. He has sent us His Spirit, the Holy (perfect) Spirit to reveal to our spirits the precise truth. He reveals to you who are willing to accept God's Word not only the inner knowing but much greater things so that you just know that the written word is exactly what God, the Almighty God, *Yahweh*, has said. The Holy Spirit always confirms the written word. God said," I am not a man that I should lie." God cannot lie, not won't, He cannot. That's what *holy* means. It's a Hebrew root word meaning "perfect". His perfect Spirit will live in us if we ask Jesus to come into our lives.

The devil sows confusion the way a farmer sows seeds in a field. The seed God sows in His Word is truth. See what Jesus has to say in Matthew 13: 36–39. That's how we can know, by the revelation of God's Word and promises, the truth that will set you free, for if you don't know the promises, you cannot claim them, and you won't be free. We can know and accept that what God has said and written is the only exact truth because we know we must accept what God has said and written as the only exact truth. Then when anyone whom the devil sends (yes, it's true) to tell you that God has taken your baby or young son, wife, husband, or best friend who has died, you can find out in God's Word that it's not God's will for you or anyone to die young, simply by reading and studying it.

Psalm 91: 16 conveys this promise from the Lord: "With long life I will satisfy you" who (see verse 2) "will say of the Lord, 'He is my refuge, my God, in whom I trust.'" Believe verse 4: "under His wings (of protection) I will find refuge, for He is my fortress, my God in whom I trust" (again from verse 2). Speak this to yourself. Psalm 91: 10 says, "No harm, no evil shall come near you or your dwelling" (your house); then verses 11 and 12 tell you why. It's because God will command His angels concerning you, to watch over you (wherever you go) in all your ways; they will hold you up in their hands so that you will not strike your foot against a stone (so that no harm will even come near you).

Then verse 13 says you – *yes, you* – will trample on lions and cobras, the great lion and the serpent. The Hebrew word for the "serpent" or "great lion" is Satan. Far from being defeated by him, you trample him by speaking commands to demons in Jesus' name. So there is just one simple promise of the covenant to those who, in verse 2, "say of the Lord, He is my refuge and my fortress, my God, in whom I trust." Notice "they say of the Lord, He is my refuge and my fortress, my God, in whom I trust " Refer to Mark 11 where Jesus tells us to speak to problems out loud. Verse 22, 23 tells us what we are to say !I tell you the truth, if anyone says to this mountain, Go, throw yourself into the sea, and does not doubt in his heart, but believes that what he says will happen, it will be done for him.

Question: Who is the Lord in Psalm 91?

Answer: See Romans 10: 8–10. This tells you that if you will believe in your heart and confess (say with your mouth) that Jesus is Lord, you shall be saved. You can be certain that the Lord, maker of heaven and earth, is Jesus, who died on a cross but rose again and is now alive. Notice that it is when you *say* or *speak* that Jesus is your Lord and refuge, your God in whom you trust, that you will be saved.

Question: Saved from what?

Answer: Hell, the devil, and his lies. Saved from all lies, deception and religious traditions, all sickness, all poverty, all wrongdoing, all depression, all loneliness, all lack and danger. Psalm 91 tells us of many of the promises of God that are for those who will say of the Lord, "He is my fortress and refuge, and under His wings I will be blessed, prospered, and protected." Notice to whom those promises are made. Those who will say out loud, "Yes, Jesus, You are God, You are alive, You died for me, but now You are alive. The Father raised You by His Spirit from the dead, and I say You will do for me all that You promised in Psalm 91."

Read it and see for yourself. God promised it all. Long life, freedom from all sickness and disease, protection for you and your entire house and family, eternal life, plus great financial blessing. Even if ten thousand fall at your side with sickness, it will not come near you (see verse 7). That's supernatural, godly protection by His power, His angels. It's true; but you have to make a quality, once-and-for-all decision to declare that God's Word and covenant promises are true to you in Christ Jesus. You need to say with your mouth what you believe God will do for you.

Question: What can you be certain God will do for you?

Answer: You can be certain He will do for you all He has said. God's Word is his will. All He has said is written in your Bible. You may be the only one in your church who believes His promises, all of them. You may be the only one in your family who believes His promises. You may be the only one in your neighbourhood whether your faith is Sikh, Hindu, Buddhist, Muslim, Jehovah's Witness, Mormon, Jew, Orthodox Jew, or Catholic. Maybe you have now decided to discard all your previous teachings and beliefs, break with all your old gods, and ask the only true God in Christ Jesus to come into your heart and confess to Him.

Confess that Jesus is Lord, and confess aloud all that Jesus has promised you. Why? Romans 10: 17 tells us that faith comes by hearing and that hearing comes by the Word of God. You need personally to hear yourself making that confession. There is nothing you can do to get eternal life by your own works or efforts. You simply accept that Jesus took all your sins (wrongdoings), all your sickness and diseases, and that by His wounds and the punishment He took in your place, you are healed (Isaiah 53:4-5 and 1 Peter 2: 24). You are now a member of God's family and heir to all the promises of God to you (in Christ), not by your own efforts but simply by trusting Jesus to do all He said. It's that simple. Do it now, please.

Let's now look at the healing promises and how to receive them in your life, your body, now, here on earth, with no tears and no pain, but with everlasting peace, joy, and prosperity. That's *Good News*. That's what resurrection means for you to experience and enjoy forever.

First, we must find the promises in the covenant (there are over 7,000 of them).

Second, we must totally believe them.

Third, we must say out loud what God has said or promised, because faith comes by hearing God's words. In the Greek the tense is a present continuous tense which means not a one-off hearing but hearing repeatedly. Then, only then, will they come into manifestation or become a reality in your body. In Mark 11: 23–24, Jesus said, "When you pray, believe you receive what you asked God for; then you shall have whatever you say." People always get what they truly believe in their hearts (spirits); they always get exactly what they say. It's true! Good or bad, it's your choice.

An example: Mr. or Mrs. Jones says, "Nothing good ever happens to us. Things always go wrong: we are the first to get flu, the first to lose our jobs, the plane breaks down before we go on holiday, the lawnmower breaks down as soon as we touch it," and so on. Notice this, they always say aloud what they believe in their hearts and think in their minds, and it always comes to pass. There is a reason. This is a spiritual law. Not law like the police arresting you for speeding or assault or robbery but like the universal law of gravity which keeps us grounded on this planet. It can't be changed, except by God overriding it with His miraculous power. You can jump all day and try to touch the moon but you will fail and you will fail again because of the law of gravity.

The Bible tells us that God has laws. One of them is the Law of the Spirit (of God). Jesus spoke of this law on many occasions and taught on it many times. Romans 8: 2 tells of two laws, a good and a bad. In Mark 11: 23 Jesus said, "If you believe you have (now) what you ask God for when you pray, you shall have whatever you say." Let's examine this closely. Remember, you have a covenant with God through the blood of Jesus. In the New Covenant, in the New Testament (the New Testament in Greek means "the last will and testament" of Jesus, God's Anointed One, the Christ), Jesus says in Mark 11: 23, "Pray, believing you have what you prayed for." God won't give you drugs to kill yourself or excessive alcohol or a weapon to kill with. If you are married, He won't give you another man or woman to have sex with. God will give you good things, anything that He has promised in His Word (over 7,000 promises). Even holidays, clothes, makeup, jewels, gold, silver, paintings, cars, houses, ships, boats, etc. He will give you these things if you will do what He says.

Read Matthew 6: 25–34, a key passage of promises and principles of God's kingdom. In verse 33 Jesus says, "Seek first the kingdom of God (God's way of doing things) and His righteousness" (you asked Jesus into your life, and you do your best to do what's right because you simply want to please God). That is: You, every one of you: Seek first God's kingdom. Don't worry if you do wrong or sin. Confess from your heart, and tell God, "Lord, I'm sorry I did this wrong today. I confess it. Please forgive me." God will forgive you and still answer your prayers. This truth is good news. I'm not telling you to do wrong, no. God's asking you not to do wrong, but if for some reason you stumble or fall, simply confess to God, "I did wrong. Forgive me, Lord, in Jesus' name," and God will forgive you.

God always answers to the name of Jesus. Yes, 1 John 1: 7–2: 2 says, Don't run away from God, your (Daddy, Father) in Christ. When you sin, when you break His word, when you do wrong, run to Him, and He will always forgive you and welcome you with open arms, always." It's in your Bible, but don't do what 1 John 1: 8 says. "If you claim to be without sin, you deceive yourselves and the truth is not in you (your mind, your memory, your heart)." So don't claim to be without sin; instead, simply go to Jesus, accept Him as Lord, ask Him into your life, and then confess you blew it many times, and He will forgive you and cleanse you of all unrighteousness. So that now makes you the righteousness of God and that's what the covenant blood (see Romans 3: 20–25) is all about. The key verse here is v22. The righteousness of God is by faith to <u>all who believe</u>. God takes all your confessed wrongs and gives you the breastplate of righteousness in place of all your sins and failures, all of them. That's *Good News*.

Read Ephesians 6: 13–18, and put on the armour that God had given you. Also, as Philippians 1: 11 says, "Be filled with the fruit of righteousness through Jesus." He will restore your relationships with your kids if you will simply ask. You need to search the Bible and find the promise you need from the 7,000-plus promises in His Word, so that you can apply Mark 11: 23 to your situation. There are many books and aids available now, especially in Christian bookshops, with a list of all the promises of God to you personally. Don't let anyone or anything rob you, especially not thoughts like *I'm not worthy* or *God won't do this or that for rubbish old me.* No, you have God's word.

Jesus Himself said, "Whosoever comes to me, I will in no way turn away" (see John 6: 37). Plus a reminder of John 3: 16 tells us that "God so loved the world (all people in it) that He (freely) gave His only Son so that whosoever believes in Him should not perish but have everlasting life." Galatians 3: 11–14 informs us that Jesus Christ died on a cross and broke the curse for us...then rose again so that the blessing (promises and prosperity) of Abraham should come to the Gentiles (all non-Jews) through Christ Jesus. Get that, all of you? That's one of the main reasons Jesus died for you, so that the promises, the blessing of Abraham, should come on you, be given to you. Also, remember we have an enemy, Satan. Read 1 John 3: 8 and Hebrews 2: 14–16, which say Jesus came to destroy the works and power of Satan and deliver all who are subject to his bondage (in slavery to Satan). He has destroyed Satan's power by His death and resurrection and delivered us who were once Satan's slaves.

Question: Delivered us from what?

Answer: Jesus delivered us from sin. Jesus delivered us from the bondage of Satan's power and destroyed his works. He delivered us from sin and the tyranny and bondage Satan uses to oppress people.

Question: If Satan's power is destroyed, why are we still subject to his bondage and oppression, to hell, sickness, lack, depression, and a lack of truth or knowledge? Why especially are those who confess to belong to Jesus Christ, seemingly still in bondage or oppression of sickness?

Answer: They are all the curses of the Law stated in the Deuteronomy 28: 15–68 (read these curses). Yet Galatians 3: 13–14 it says, "Christ Jesus became a curse for us, so that Abraham's blessing might come on the people of the world (Gentiles) through Jesus Christ." Jesus in His death and resurrection defeated death and broke the curse so that all people could be blessed through Him. Jesus is a mighty blessing.

Question: So why are even many Christians, even good living ones, still dying young, their kids sick or dying, still lacking money, food, clothes, or dwellings, still short of peace, living in fear of the devil and fear that God might not help?

Answer: Lack of knowledge of God's instructions and lack of faith. Hosea 4: 6 tells us it's a lack of knowledge of God's Word, commands, and promises, plus a lack of faith in those promises. That's all, nothing more or less. It is that simple.

Question: What is the remedy?

Answer: For you to get more knowledge and more faith, you need to get more knowledge of God's promises to you and learn how to get more faith in His Word. So now let's get down to practical business: how to put these principles to work in your life. Everything comes through knowing what God has said. What He has said is His will. Faith in His Word comes by you hearing yourself speaking God's promises and hearing others speaking God's Word. Romans 10: 17 explains it: faith comes by hearing and hearing by continually or daily reading and hearing God's Word. You must do the above to receive His promises. It's by having knowledge of God, His Word, and His promises and by having faith or trust in His love and ability to perform His Word.

Question: How are you born again or saved?

Answer: Someone preached or spoke God's Word to you. Someone told you to ask Jesus into your life, right? Certainly! So how did your faith in Jesus come? By hearing and hearing someone speak or preach God's promise, as stated in Romans 10: 8–10: If you believe in your heart and confess with your mouth, that Jesus died for you and that He is now alive, raised from the dead, you will be saved, go to heaven, and receive eternal life. You believe it because it was first spoken; second, you heard it; and third, you believed it. Some of you were saved by reading Romans 10: 8–10, and you confessed with your mouth Jesus as your Lord, Master, and Saviour. This is one of God's promises.

In fact, this is how to receive any of God's promises. Mark 11: 23 is a major law of the Spirit. Pray, and you shall have whatever you say (good or bad). The process is always the same: first, you hear a promise of God, any promise; second, you believe what you say and hear yourself saying aloud, then, third, you say, "I now have it". If for instance, you lack a home or money, find one of God's promises about houses or money. Remember, you are only repeating what God has already said or promised you. That's what He said will come to pass in your life. Praise God, it will. That's receiving or experiencing what you believe and say.

Hebrews 11: 1, in the King James Version says, "Faith is the substance of things (you) hoped for (when you prayed and said you had it), the evidence of things not (yet) seen." In the New International Version of the Bible (NIV), Hebrews 11: 1 is translated into English as, "Now faith is being sure of what we hope for and certain of what we do not yet see." When people ask you how you are (when you are believing God for healing), you must speak health and well-being, but especially say it to yourself daily, because you will get what you say continually.

Genesis 1: 1–31 says all things were put here, were created, after God spoke. God said, "Let there be light." The light was or came. God said, "Let there be an expanse (between the waters – a sky) over earth." And the sky was. God said, "Let the waters under the sky be gathered together." Then the waters were gathered together, and dry land appeared. God said, "Let the land produce vegetation." Vegetation then came.

After you read Genesis 1: 1–31, then read Hebrews 11: 3, which explains Genesis 1: 1–3: "By faith in God's word we understand that the universe was formed at God's command (words) so that what is seen was not made out of what was visible" (NIV). Praise God! See it? It's a spiritual law. God said, "Universe, be." After He said it, the universe was formed out of the substance that is inside God. When God spoke, the substance took upon itself the form of what God desired. Faith is the substance of things we expect, hope for, the evidence of things not (yet) seen. Do you see it? Open their spiritual eyes, Lord.

Can you see the air? No. Can you see the atoms and molecules with your physical eyes? No. Can you see magnetic waves or electricity with your natural eyes? No. Yet you know these particles and powers and forces exist or are there – both because they can be detected or measured scientifically on certain meters or visual devices, radio telescopes, spectrometers, etc.; and by experience. We breathe unseen air. If you take a magnet and pull a nail towards it without it touching, you know magnetic force is there and works. Yet it's unseen.

This is how your faith in Jesus and His Word works: unseen, yet it's there always. God watches over His Word, His promises, to perform them or carry them out (Jer. 1: 12).

Question: When does God perform His Word that He watches over?

Answer: When you, one of His children, believe in Jesus and His Word and *say* that you have what God has promised, that's when God hears you. He promised He will watch over His Word, and He will perform it, bring it into existence, because you believe in God's ability to bring it to pass. It is that simple. It's now up to you to find the promises and tell God that you believe Him.

Next I'll give you a list of Scriptures, promises on faith (to read in your own time), and then we will move on to the healing promises found in God's Word. They are faith-filled confessions that you simply have to say aloud on a daily basis and believe in your heart. It takes time, but it works every time. In this chapter the promises of God are on healing and knowing your enemy, Satan – how you can bind him, tie him up, and render him and the demons and all their curses of sickness, poverty, fear, confusion, deception, etc., of *no effect* in your life.

Read on. Learn more of what's yours and what great power and control you have in Christ. Put the past behind you. Turn around, away from fear and defeat; turn to faith and victory from now on. Forgive yourself. Ask God to forgive you (for what you thought He had allowed or brought on you). Forgive your friends, family, enemies (by God's power and Spirit), and with His help go *free!*

Now read Mark 11: 23–24.

First, read the Scriptures about trust or faith in God, Jesus, His Word, and His promises. Take the time to read them in your own Bible. Then move on to the promises of your God-given authority over Satan and over all the curses of the law that are found in Deuteronomy 28: 15–68. The Good News is located in Deuteronomy 28: 1–14; it's a list of God's promises to you as Abraham's seed. In church circles (those who know the promises of God), verses 1–14 are known as Abraham's Blessings or Abraham's Promises (from God to him and his seed forever). You are Abraham's seed, in Christ the Anointed One. Those promises and commands are all yours, so find them, read them, and claim them, telling

God with your mouth, "I am Abraham's seed; these promises are mine. Thank You, Lord. I claim them all now, in Jesus' name."

All the good works in the world will not get you eternal life or a place in heaven, healing, or freedom from demons or oppression. But faith, trust in God and His Word (promises), will. Without *faith* in God and His Word (what God has said), it is impossible to please God, says Hebrews 11: 6. The just, or those whom God has made righteousness *in* Christ, will live by faith (in God and His Word). They are justified. Habakkuk 2: 4, Romans 1: 17, and Galatians 3: 11 all tell us this. This is how we overcome the world (all its evils): by our faith (trust in God and His promises) and God's ability to bring His promises to pass (see 1 John 5: 4).

Matthew 9: 29 says, "According to your faith it will be done unto you (simply believe God's promise and it will be done for you)." Also, in Matthew 17: 20 we read, "If you have faith small as a mustard seed (tiny) you can say to a mountain or to a big problem, go, be cast into the sea, and the mountain will obey you." It's your command spoken in Jesus' name. Then Jesus said in Luke 7: 9, "in all of Israel, I have not found (in a man) such great faith (or trust in God)." In this account a Roman centurion is the man who said, "Speak the word only, and my servant shall be healed." He understood the authority of the spoken word and so didn't need Jesus to come and lay His hands on his servant. Jesus' Word was sufficient. Faith impresses God, and it impresses the Lord Jesus!

Faith Promises

- Luke 17: 5 – He will increase our faith.
- Luke 18: 8 – Will Jesus find faith on earth when He returns (people who actually believe His promises)?
- Acts 14: 9 – Paul saw that the crippled man had faith to be healed.
- Acts 14: 27 – The door to faith (Jesus is the door).
- Romans 1: 12 – Encourage each other's faith.
- Romans 1: 17 – Faith (in God and His Word) from first to last.
- Romans 1: 17 – The righteous are those who have faith in God (to do what He has said).

- Romans 3: 22 – Righteousness comes through faith in Jesus Christ.
- Ephesians 6: 16 –You take up the shield of faith as part of God's armour.
- Hebrews 11: 6 – "Without faith it is impossible to please God, because anyone who comes to Him must believe that He exists and that He rewards those who earnestly seek Him." (NIV)
- John 6: 28–29 – What must we do to do the works of God? Believe on the one (Jesus) who God YHWH sent.
- Romans 10: 17 – Faith comes through hearing, and hearing (comes) through the Word of God.

There are many, many more promises on faith. Seek them out in your Bible, you will find them. Simply take the time daily to look. What's one hour a day for reading God's Word? People spend all day watching TV, reading books, doing hobbies, playing sports, or just listening to the radio. Come on, we generally do what we want to. Weigh up the benefits to be gained and the losses to be avoided, great losses. When you spend time in God's Word and pray, asking God to reveal to you exactly what each promise really means and then trusting Him to speak back to you inside your spirit as He promised, He will do it. Prayer means communication with God, speaking and then being quiet and waiting for Him to answer you, to speak back to you. When you ask God to explain His Word to you, what it really means, be assured He has heard you. He's alive and He's there in you (if you asked Jesus into your life), so because He's there in you, His Spirit in you will speak Spirit to spirit – from His Spirit direct to yours. There is no error in what God says and there is no error in what you hear. That's why God communicates Spirit to spirit rather than through an audible voice, because when people speak to one another, there may be errors, mistakes. or misinformation in what's spoken and heard.

Since God is omniscient (all-knowing), He can only speak exact (accurate) knowledge. To ensure that you fully understand what He exactly said, in the way He wanted you to hear it, He speaks not to your body or brain but directly to the real you, your spirit, which lives in your body. If you are born again, your spirit is recreated by the power of God's Spirit (that happened when you asked Jesus into your life). Your reborn spirit is exactly like God's Spirit. So now you hear in your spirit and understand in your spirit exactly what God means when He speaks (into you). Then, following this, you understand it in your mind. There is a substance there called faith, see Hebrews 11:1 (in God and His Word), and whenever you read something God has said, it automatically triggers a knowledge inside you that confirms this is exact revealed truth. The Bible calls this *rhema* knowledge.

As 1 Corinthians 2: 9 says, "Eye has not seen nor ear heard what God has already prepared as an inheritance for those that love Him." Verse 10 declares "it has been revealed to us (in Christ) by His Spirit (the Holy Spirit)," the perfect Spirit, without error or fault, omniscient (knowing everything). That's Good News. Acts 1: 4, 7–8 says, "Stay in Jesus. You will receive the promise (promised Holy Spirit or anointing), and you will be clothed, covered, baptised with power from on high." The disciples experienced the Spirit of God coming on each of them; they were anointed with burden-removing, yoke-destroying power. Isaiah 10: 27 states that the anointing is to destroy and remove all the power of Satan and all the curses, all the sickness, lack, poverty, debt and lack of knowledge.

You can now start to learn who you really are in Christ, as God's covenant child. Like Father, like son. As you study God's Word daily, you will grow in stature to be exactly like God and Jesus in image. You start to realise that what belongs to you, freely given by God, is reality, not myth. You begin to see and experience covenant blessings now on earth with your physical body. They come to pass or manifest. Read Matthew 21: 18–22, Mark 11: 20–26, and Mark 5: 25–34. There are many more examples in the Bible of saying it and then seeing it. These are just a few examples, but wonderful examples of health returning after simply believing God's Word and by saying one receives what one desired and confessed, such as the woman with the issue of blood in Mark 5: 25–34. The key verse 28 says, "For she said, 'If I just touch the hem of His garments, I shall be made whole'" (complete, nothing missing). She went, she said it, she did it (touched Him), and then the power flowed into her.

She gave testimony, and Jesus said, "Woman, go thy way, your faith (in God's promises, God's word) has made you whole." Can you see it? Her faith in what Jesus said He would do for anyone who came to Him made her whole. Yes, recognise that she had heard. Just the way a magnet draws iron to it, her faith drew the healing power of Jesus into her, and that power drove all sickness out and repaired and restored her body to perfection. Notice Jesus did not say His faith had made her well. He said her trust in Him to do what He promised for anyone who came to Him, this is what made her well again. That's Good News!

Luke 4: 17–21 continues to proclaim the year of the Lord's abundant, free favour. Now read Isaiah 61: 1–2. This Old Testament prophecy told, approximately 750 years before Jesus came, that the Anointed One would come in the future.

Luke 4: 17–21 tells us that the Anointed One has now come, and His name is Jesus. Verse 21 says Jesus began (his job, his mission, ministry) by saying, "Today (now) is this scripture (Isaiah 61: 1–2) fulfilled."

Question: How did He do it?

Answer: With the anointing power.

Question: How did the power flow?

Answer: These are our weapons that work every time, by words of faith. When Jesus spoke aloud, "Leper, be whole," the power to heal (the anointing) flowed into the leper and brought to pass exactly what Jesus believed in His heart would happen. He always said what He believed in His heart, and what He believed in His heart, He always said aloud.

Question: Why?

Answer: Because this is a law of the Spirit which releases the power flow. That's just the way it is, or as a singer from the sixties and early 1970s sang, "That's the way God planned it; that's the way God wants it to be." It's the law of the Spirit of Life; that's the way God Himself does it. He believes He can do it. He speaks it, and then it appears – it comes to pass.

Question: What has this got to do with you?

Answer: Read Mark 16: 14–18. Jesus did all these great works with the Anointing power of God on Him, and when He spoke, the devils left and the sickness was healed. What has this got to do with you? Jesus said to His disciples in verse 15, "Go into all the world and preach the Good News, and whoever believes will be saved." Verse 17 says, "And these signs shall follow whosoever believes (in Jesus and what He said): they shall cast out devils." Verse 18 says, "They shall lay hands on the sick, and the sick shall recover." No deadly poisons, insects, snakes, etc., shall hurt you.

Do you see it? Jesus said it, that those who believe in Him will have the same signs, miracles, and power following them. *You* shall cast demons out. *You* shall lay hands on the sick, and in Jesus' name, they shall recover. Again, speaking of us in Jesus Christ, Revelation 12: 10–11 says, "This is how they (God's people) overcome the evil one (the devil, demons), by the blood of the Lamb (Jesus) and speaking their testimony out of their mouth."

Do you see it? Jesus, who gave His blood for *you* (*you* have a covenant), has given promises to *you* that these signs shall follow *you*. *You* shall cast out the devil (and his sickness, poverty, etc.) from *your* life. Now, glory. *You* have been given the name above all names, Jesus, to use. Use it by speaking aloud. *You* have been given the blood (of the New Covenant), making *you* heir to all Jesus had and has. *You*, in God's sight, have the right to use the power, the anointing of the Holy Spirit, by using *your* mouth to declare aloud God's promises, saying the promise audibly in Jesus' name, "God promised me in the Word of God, by the blood of the Lamb, Jesus, sacrificed for me."

Based on John 14: 12–14, you can say, "Whatever I ask of Him, He will do for me. I'm saying now, 'house, come' or 'sickness (name the sickness), go, in Jesus' name."

"Cancer, lack, poverty, you're a mountain, and Jesus said in Mark 11: 23 that if I say to the mountain, be cast into the sea, it will obey me." It's my God-given right in Jesus to command cancer, illness, headaches, and the like be cast into the sea. So say, "Satan, all sickness is oppression of the devil. Acts 10: 38 says so. Luke 10: 19 says that I have all authority over the enemy and all his power of curses. So I say, Satan, take yourself and your sickness (trouble, name them), your mountains, and go forever from me and never return, in the name of Jesus and for His glory. Amen." You shall have whatsoever you say as long as you say it in Jesus' name.

Each day spend time with God, reading your covenant, God's Word, and develop your love for God Himself. Pray or talk to God, asking Him to reveal to you what your reading actually means. As best you can, do what's loving and right. Be kind to everyone, poor as well as rich. That is to seek first the kingdom of God. Search for the promises daily in your Bible; it's exciting, it's true, it's fun, and it brings victory, peace, and love to you and many others in your life – family, friends, children, the poor, the homeless, and the Christian ministries to whom you give out of your blessings, the prosperity given to you by God through your faith in Him and His promises. *The more you have, the more you can give to those to whom God leads you* and to those you love, as well as enjoying lots of good things yourself; that's okay with Jesus. The more money you have, the more you can give. The more peace you have, the more you can give. The more knowledge of God you have, the more you can give. The more power you have from God, the more you can give. The more joy you have, the more you can give. God's law is, the more you have, the more you share it with Him and others.

God's promises spoken in faith are mighty weapons against Satan. Ephesians 6: 17 tells us that the Word of God is the sword of the Spirit and is part of God's armour. Taken with verse 16, the shield of faith is like a shield of defence against Satan's weapons, and speaking God's Word is like a sword against Satan and his weaponry. Read Ephesians 6: 10–18 to hear about all the other armour of God (breastplate = righteousness, helmet = salvation, and the rest). In God's eyes, you are righteous immediately after you ask Jesus into your life.

For now we will concentrate on the sword and the shield. The shield stands for your trust in what God says, His promises. The sword represents declaring God's words aloud for yourself and against the devil. In doing this you have now put yourself totally in God's loving hands for your healing or any other need you have. Just like going to a medical surgeon for an operation, you allow the surgeon to give you an anaesthetic to put you to sleep. Then, whilst you are unconscious, you trust him to use his scalpel and instruments to perform the necessary procedure. You put yourself in the doctor's total control and fully trust him to perform a successful operation and stitch you up afterwards.

This is the way you come to Jesus. You say, "Lord, I'm declaring aloud your promises on healing daily, and I fully expect and believe You to do what You said and promised, knowing in my heart and spirit that you are a loving, kind God, who will do all I ask of you according to your Word." That's faith, trust in God and what He said. This is your shield. Then as you say out loud the promises, this is your sword against the devil, sickness, and fear.

It works. God's medicine is His Word. Read Proverbs 4: 20–22. Don't try and figure out how you will get well, just take the medicine daily. God's medicine is saying aloud what God's Word declares. Just do it! Believe it, and know God will do it. Healing and miracles, both are from our heavenly Father.

To finish this chapter, you need to know there is a difference between receiving a healing from God and receiving a miracle. Let me briefly explain. Be patient, the more knowledge you have about God and His promises, the more confident or trusting you will become.

First, let's deal with receiving a healing from Jesus. Let's look at a few examples. If you have a cancer or a disease, you need to be healed of this; you need God's power to destroy the microbes, germs, bacteria, etc. This is healing. If you have a hole in your heart or a part of your body, such as a limb, finger, toe, or an internal organ missing or damaged beyond repair, you need God to replace the old or damaged organs or limb with a new one: to create a new finger, organ, or limb to grow anew. This is a job for a miracle. A miracle is something which cannot happen naturally. Your body's natural healing process does not include regenerating new parts or filling holes in your heart or brain, so a miracle is needed.

A miracle is defined (as God's word exactly means) as something that happens which defies natural, physical, or scientific laws .If someone had lost a limb in an accident years ago and then the new limb appeared suddenly, that would be a miracle, going against all natural, human, biological law. God is able to do and has done many miracles. The Bible records many miracles where God used His supernatural power to do things which naturally could never happen. Luke 1: 37 (NIV) says, "Nothing is impossible with God." Matthew 17: 20 says, "Nothing is impossible to him who believes (in God and His Word and promises"), and Luke 18: 27 declares, "What's impossible to men is possible with God."

Your job, if you need a miracle, is to say, "Lord, I believe this. Nothing is impossible to me so I'm saying, make whole this heart or lung or arm or leg or spine, etc. Or make whole these wasted legs and get me out of this wheelchair." Yes, Jesus did and still does miracles today, lots of them. See Ephesians 3: 20, where it says, "God will do for you immeasurably more than you can ask or imagine, according to the power that works in us." That's God's healing power. If you have something which is impossible for doctors or scientists to cure, ask God to make you whole, complete, with everything restored, regrown, or regenerated, and then say daily, "Thanks, Lord. I'm whole, according to your promises in Luke 1: 37, Matthew 17: 20, Luke 18: 27 and Ephesians 3: 20." These words are your weapons and defence against sickness, calamity, and even impossible situations.

God will always give you a way out of every trial, test or temptation that demons or life can throw at you and you will not have to bear more than you are able. Read God's promise in 1 Corinthians 10: 13. All tests, trials, troubles, and temptations are from Satan, *not* from God. God is not sending you any trial or test, such as an illness or poverty, not depression or missing limbs, nor deformity, pain, or agony, nor sin of any kind. Read James 1: 13 which says, "Don't let anyone say when he is tried or tested, it is the Lord, for the Lord tests (tries) no one. Nor is He (God) tried or tested by anyone." So let no one say or believe falsely that your misery or torment or lack is from God. *It is not.* God is not putting anyone through trials and tests. The devil and demons are, and if you know this, you can now resist the devil and all his evils – sickness, troubles, and poverty – and the devil and all his curses will flee (run, go away) from you! However, this is only if you resist him and his oppressions. James 4: 7–8 says, "Submit yourselves to God (by believing and obeying His word) and resist (refuse to accept) the devil (and his evils and troubles and sin)." Say it in Jesus' name, and Satan will, he *must* flee from you. From whom? From *you!*

See 3 John 2, which says, "Dear friends, I pray above all things that you may enjoy good health and that you may prosper (that all will go well for you) even as your soul (mind, will and emotions) is prospering (receiving more knowledge of God, his teachings, commands and promises) and that your (mind) will (increase in the knowledge of God)." Prosper as you believe. In 1 John 5: 13–15, verse 14 says, "If we ask him for anything according to His will (God's will is His Word, His promises) written down, then we know that He hears us and (verse 15) that we have what we asked Him for."

Today, speak to your mountain of impossibilities (sickness, disability, poverty), and say in Jesus' name, "Be cast out into the sea, flee from me." Say, "Satan, take yourself and your curses and sickness from me now." He will flee from you. Lastly, don't allow anyone to tell you that it is God allowing this suffering to come to you. No! No one! God's not allowing it;

you are! However, now you can stop it. You can now say, "Sickness (name it), I'm not allowing you in my body any longer. I'm going free today, in Jesus' name! Amen."

Now go to chapter 4 of this book, and say aloud the Healing Promises. Say them daily. Take the Word (God's medicine) into your ears, into your heart daily. The enemy, with his sickness, poverty, and destruction, will flee from you. Believe God's promises. That's your job, to believe God's Word from the Bible. You now know it is the enemy, the tempter, the tester, the devil, who brings trials. You now know it's not God, and it never was.

You now know you have weapons given to you by God, in Jesus' name. Now choose to use them. Do it, choose life. Deuteronomy 30: 19–20 says, "Choose you this day, life or death, blessing or cursing. Therefore, says the Lord God, choose life and God's blessings." The choice is yours. Make the intelligent choice. Dear reader, the desire of my heart is that you choose to take long life in all its fullness and prosperity, for the glory of Jesus Christ. Amen.

CHAPTER 4

COVENANT HEALING

The Covenant and the Healing Promises

So now you know the enemy, don't listen to his lies. Let's look at the various ways to receive healing or miracles of restoration. The Number One way with God is by you speaking the promises and receiving them by *faith*, by your *covenant* with *God!*

First, you read, think, and meditate on the promises.

Second, you say out loud the confessions. You hang on to them above all else, for dear life! This is God's best way. Faith comes by hearing.

Third, you can receive healing by going to some men or women who are in Christ and ask them to anoint (put oil) on you and, in Jesus' name, pray for your healing, and God will heal you as you believe this promise. Jesus will forgive all your sin then and there. Read James 5: 14–16 in your Bible. You can go to any true believer in Jesus and His promises, ask them to lay hands on you and pray for your healing, and you will recover. Read Mark 16: 17–18.

Fourth, if you need a miracle to receive something humanly impossible (we dealt with the definition of a miracle in the last chapter), you can pray and ask God for it yourself or pray and ask God to put you in touch with a person who has been given the gift of working miracles in Jesus' name. Read 1 Corinthians 12: 9–10. You can watch preachers and their meetings on the television's Christian channels.

Now we will concentrate on the most practical way to receive healing or a miracle in your own body or body of a loved one, friend or acquaintance. *Remember this.* When you go to the doctor or hospital, and the doctor prescribes medicine or pills, he tells you to take the medicine, say, twice each day until it's all gone. Only when you have taken the medicine can you expect to start feeling and actually getting well again. You would not just say, "I know that if I take the medicine, I will get better, but I will just leave it on the shelf and look at it." No, you would not get well. You would have to *obey, carry out the instructions* of the doctor. In God's way of doing things written in the Bible, it's the same. You must obey God's instructions concerning how to be healed or how to receive financial prosperity or anything you desire (that's promised to you) in the Word of God..

Question: What is God's medicine and how do I take it?

Answer: God's medicine is His Word, His promises. You speak aloud the promises. As you hear them go into your spirit, the heart of your being, *faith* comes by hearing. Don't try to figure out how God's Word will work. Simply take the medicine of God's Word daily. *Do it*, and it will work for you!

The *key to life* and death, sickness or health is Hosea 4: 6, which says that God's people perish or are destroyed from lack of knowledge, understanding of His Word. Either they don't know they have a covenant with God, or they just don't do what they should do – that is, take the medicine! Now here is how you do it daily. Proverbs 4: 20–22 says, "My son, attend to my word; incline your ears to my sayings. Do not let them depart from your eyes; keep them in the midst of your heart because they are life unto those that find them and health (medicine) unto all your flesh (body)." The Hebrew word for "health" in verse 22 literally means medicine, so God's medicine is His Word, and His Word is the medicine God prescribes for all your (body) flesh.

You need to believe God's Word is His medicine, look at the promises daily, and say them out loud daily so that they go from your mouth into your ears and into your spirit, your heart, and your body. Get the written promises out before your eyes, speak them out loud, and believe your body is being healed and made whole as you are hearing the promises. This is how you put God's medicine on a spoon, open your mouth, and swallow it. God's Word is His medicine.

Here are several examples or parallels between God's Word and natural medicine (prescribed by your GP). God's Word is a healing agent just as natural medicine is a healing agent or catalyst which helps your body's natural defences against disease, aiding your white corpuscles. God's Word contains within itself the capacity to produce healing and wholeness.

- **Proverbs 4: 20, 22** – My son, attend to my words; … for they are life to those that find them and health and medicine to all their flesh.
- **Hebrews 4: 12** – The word of God is quick and powerful and sharper than any two-edged sword, cutting, piercing, even dividing asunder soul and spirit (and joint or bone or marrow).
- **Isaiah 55: 10–11** – The Word of God will accomplish exactly what it was sent to do.
- **Psalm 107: 20** – He sent His Word and healed them and delivered them from (all) their destructions (and corruptions). He sent His Word, and it healed and freed them!

The key to partaking of the life and healing of God's Word is to feed on it until it penetrates into your spirit, where it deposits the life and healing energy. This happens through saying it and believing it. We could say that the medicine is no respecter of persons. It plays no favourites; it will work for anyone who takes it. It is not a matter of whether God is willing or unwilling to heal. *God is willing!* Most importantly, the medicine (God's Word) must be taken according to the exact instructions in order to be effective. Head knowledge or intellectual knowledge (simply knowing about healing) won't do. God's words, His promises, are going to have to penetrate into your spirit as a result of meditating on them, seeing, hearing, and speaking them with belief to produce healing or wholeness in your body. You can see God's way of healing is spiritual. His Spirit and His words are transferred into your spirit and then from your spirit into your body. God's medicine must be taken internally, through the mouth by saying it aloud.

Below is a list of healing Scriptures, God's promises. Feed on them several times a day; little and often will do. The medicine will work if you get it inside yourself. Remember that it takes time for the medicine to work. Most people will give natural medicine time to work. Time, patience, and money are required to go back to the pharmacy for refills. They are diligent about it. So keep on taking God's medicine; give it time to work. Speak the Scriptures to yourself. Think on what you are saying (in your heart). Praise your Father God. His Word is medicine, health to your flesh.

Now the promises. Read them, think on them, mull over them, and then say aloud the confession of your faith in God and His promises. It's up to you now.

- **Exodus 15: 25–26** – And Moses cried unto the Lord and the Lord showed him a tree which when he had cast into the waters, the waters were made sweet. There he made for them a statute and an ordinance (command and promise), and there he proved them and said, if you will diligently hearken unto the voice of the Lord your God and will do that which is right in His sight and will give ear to His commandments and keep all His statutes, I will not allow any of these diseases upon you which were upon the Egyptians, for I am the Lord that healeth thee.

Speak the confessions below:

"My God is speaking to me now, saying, "I am the Lord that heals thee." He is watching over His word to perform it. He is the Lord that healeth me. He is healing me now. This word contains the ability to produce what it says. His word is full of healing power. I receive the healing that is in His word *now*. God is on me. My body is the temple of God. My body is the temple of the Lord that healeth me! God is bigger than sickness and Satan. God is dwelling inside me now! God is healing me now. The Lord that healeth me is my Shepherd; I do not lack healing. My body is in contact with the Lord that healeth me. My body has to respond to God's healing power. Healing is in God, and God is in me. I thank you, Father, because You are my healer, and You are healing me now. Amen."

- **Deuteronomy 7: 15** – The Lord will keep from me all sickness and allow none of the diseases of Egypt upon me Amen.
- **Psalm 30: 2** – Oh Lord, my God, I cried unto thee and thou hast healed me.

I believe I have received my healing (or miracle). Thou hast healed me. I don't consider what I feel; I believe I am healed – Thou hast healed me. I have what I say according to Mark 11: 23. I say to the mountain (sickness, name it!), Be cast into the sea. I have what I say! I refuse to be cast down or discouraged. I am the conqueror; I praise Him who is the health of my countenance and my God. Father, I praise You. Amen.

- **Psalm 91: 1–16** – Speak aloud all of Psalm 91 each day to receive the protection of Almighty God and His angels and long life and good health. All its promises. Read it and speak it aloud in faith.

"I am abiding under the shadow of the Almighty. Jehovah Rapha, the Lord that healeth me, is my refuge and fortress against disease. His Word is my shield and buckler against sickness. Under His wings there is healing (Malachi 4: 2). I'm not afraid of disease and sickness. I'm abiding under the shadow of the Almighty, Jehovah Rapha, the Lord who heals me. No plague shall come near my dwelling or my body. I resist sickness and disease; I refuse to accept it, it's not mine. I refuse to be sick, in Jesus' name. Sickness cannot trespass in my body. Sickness (name it, name them), you can't come nigh my dwelling. I refuse, I resist you, in Jesus' name. Amen."

- **Psalm 103: 1–22** – Speak all of Psalm 103 every day. There are many promises for wholeness, renewal of your youth, and your desires being satisfied, to name a few.

Say aloud this faith confession: "Bless the Lord Jehovah Rapha, O my soul; blessed be God the Father. Lord, I praise You. Lord, I thank You. I worship You for all Your benefits. You forgive me of all my sin, all my failures, and my disobedience; You heal all my diseases, and I thank You for it. Healing belongs to me as part of the New Covenant. Healing is my redemptive right, a benefit which is a condition of a contract. Thank You, Father God, for healing me of all my diseases."

- **Psalm 107:19-20** they cried to the Lord in their trouble and He saved them from their trouble(distress) He sent His Word and healed them and delivered them from their destruction.

Say this aloud in faith: "He sent His Word and healed me; His word heals me and delivers me from my destruction. His Word frees me from my corruption. God's Word contains God's ability to perform what it says (Isaiah 55: 10–11). His Word is healing me now; His Word contains His healing power. He has sent His Word and healed me. Amen."

Say aloud this faith confession: "God's Word is health to all my flesh. The Word of God is full of the life of God. That life is saturating my spirit and is at work in me now. That life and health is spreading out of my spirit into every tissue, pore, organ, bone, and joint of my body, creating health and soundness. My body has no choice but to respond to the healing in the word that is being absorbed into me now. Amen."

- **Proverbs 12: 18** – "There is a tongue that speaks like the piercing of a sword: but the tongue of the wise is health."

Thoughtless words can wound as deeply as any sword, but wisely spoken words can heal. There are some whose uncontrolled talk is like the wounds of a sword, but the tongue of the wise man makes a person well again.

Say aloud this faith confession: "My tongue makes me well. I have what I say. I say the Word is my healer. He takes sickness away from me. No plague can come near my dwelling. I say He heals all my diseases. What I confess, I possess. My words make me well. There is healing power in my words, for they are God's words. I speak health to every muscle, tissue, and fibre in my body. I release God's healing power into my whole body. Thank you, Jesus. Amen."

- **Proverbs 17: 22** – "A merry heart doeth good like a medicine: but a broken spirit dries the bones."

In other words, if you keep your heart merry, it will bring healing to all your flesh, but a heart full of worry brings body malfunctions; this is spiritual law. So choose not to worry. Choose instead to be merry, knowing the medicine of God's Word is making you well as you speak it. A glad heart makes a healthy body.

Say aloud this faith confession: (Don't feel silly, this works! Just do it!) "Ha, ha, ha, ha! I have a merry heart. Sickness, you can't dominate me. Satan, demons, you can't dominate me. In Jesus' name, I resist you. God said to resist the devil and he will flee, he will run from me; so take your sickness with you *now!* You can't put sickness on me. I'm full of joy! Ha, ha, ha, ha, ha! A merry heart does me good just like medicine. God's Word, His medicine, is working in me now. Amen."

- **Isaiah 53: 3–5** – "He is despised and rejected of men; a man of sorrows, and acquainted with grief: and we hid as it were our faces from Him; He was despised, and we esteemed Him not. Surely He has borne our griefs, and carried our sorrows: yet we did esteem him stricken, smitten of God, and afflicted. But He was wounded for our transgressions, He was bruised for our iniquities: the chastisement of our peace was upon Him; and with His stripes we are healed."

Say aloud this faith confession: "Surely He (Jesus) has borne my sickness and diseases and carried my pains. He bore them and carried them away. I don't have to bear what He bore for me. I refuse to bear what He bore for me. Satan, in Jesus' name, you cannot put on me what Jesus bore for me. By His stripes, I am healed; by His stripes, I got healing. By His bruises, there is healing for me. His punishment has brought me healing. Healing has been granted for me with the stripes that wounded Him. I am healed and made whole (perfected health). I am made whole by the blows He received. My diseases went to the cross with Jesus and died with Him there. Satan, you are visiting the wrong person. In Jesus' name, I cast out demons. I lay hands on the sick, and they recover. These signs follow me. I'm a believer, and Mark 16: 14–18 says so. It's God's promise to me, in Christ. Jesus took my sickness, and by His stripes, I am healed. Amen."

- **Malachi 4: 2** – "But unto you that fear my name (Yahweh – in English, Jehovah and Jesus) shall the Sun of Righteousness arise with healing in His wings; and ye shall go forth, and grow up as calves of the stall."

Say this faith confession aloud: "The Son of God, the Sun of Righteousness, has arisen, having conquered sickness and Satan. There is healing in His wings; that healing power is beaming sun-like rays into me now, by His words that I speak. I am trusting beneath His healing wings."

- **Matthew 8: 2–3** – And behold, there came a leper and worshipped Him (Jesus), saying, "Lord, if you wish, you can make me clean." And Jesus put forth His hand and touched him, saying, "I will, be thou (made) clean," and immediately his leprosy was cleansed.

Say this faith confession aloud: "God wants me well. Healing was always the will of Jesus. Healing is the will of God. God is at work in me right now to will and to do His good pleasure because Philippians 2: 13 says so. Healing is at work in me now. Praise God."

- **Matthew 8: 16–17** – When the evening was come, they brought unto Him many that were possessed with devils and He cast out the spirits with His Word and healed all that were sick, that it might be fulfilled which was spoken by Esaias (Isaiah) the prophet, saying, He (Jesus the Christ) took upon himself our infirmities and bore our sicknesses.

Say this faith confession aloud: "Satan, In Jesus' name, you can't bind me with sickness or infirmity because I have been delivered from your power and domination and translated into the kingdom of the Son of God (Colossians 1: 13). Sickness is ungodly. Sickness is of you, Satan, and you can't put sickness on me or keep it on me. Who do you think you are? The Bible says you are a defeated enemy. Jesus stripped you of your authority over me. Colossians 2: 14–15 and Hebrews 2: 14–15 declare it. You can't do this to me! I resist you in Jesus' name and by the blood of the Lamb (Revelation 12: 11). So I apply His blood, which brings Abraham's blessings to me, and in His name, which has all authority over you and all demons and all your powers, I say, I am delivered, I am free, I have been loosed, I am no longer fettered or in bondage. I am rid of infirmity. My bondage is at an end. It is right for me to be completely healed, for I am a child of Abraham, and Abraham's blessings are mine (Galatians 3: 14 says so). Healing is part of the covenant, and I am under the covenant! Healing is a covenant right (Psalm 103: 3 says so). It's one of my benefits. I will not forget any of my covenant benefits. Healing is mine, because healing has been given to me. It is my rightful possession. I have a right to be released. Satan, in Jesus' name, by the blood of the Lamb, I demand my rights *now*. Take your filthy hands off my body."

Say aloud this faith statement: "Sickness is oppression of the devil. Satan, you can't oppress me with sickness because I have been delivered from your authority (Colossians 1: 13 says so). Satan, you can't oppress me because I have authority over you to cast out demons (Mark 16: 17 says so), and I have authority to tread on Satan and demons and over all the power of the enemy (Satan, demons, sickness); Luke 10: 19 says so. I tread on sickness, Satan, in the mighty name of Jesus. Amen."

- **Romans 8: 2** – For the law of the Spirit of life in Christ Jesus has made me free from the law of sin and of death.
- **Romans 8: 11** – "If the spirit of Him that raised up Jesus from the dead dwell in you, He that raised up (Jesus) Christ (the Anointed One) from the dead shall also quicken your mortal bodies by the power of His Spirit that dwelleth in you!"

Say aloud: "The Spirit of God is residing in me. He is creating life, supplying life in my body, making it whole. The life of Jehovah Rapha is being applied to my body by His Spirit who dwells in me. The life of God and His life-giving power drive out every trace of sickness and disease. The life of God is destroying disease, germs, and malfunctions in my body, right now, in the name of Jesus, for his glory. Amen."

- **1 Corinthians 6: 13, 15, 19–20 – Verse 13:** Meat for the belly and the belly (made) for meat (food) but God shall destroy both it (the belly) and them (meats, foods). Now (in the same way) the body is not (made) for fornication (sex outside Christian marriage) but the body is made for the Lord and the Lord (Jesus) for the body.

- **Verse 15:** Don't you know that your bodies are the members (parts) of (Jesus) Christ? Shall I then take the members (parts) of Christ and make them the members of a harlot (prostitute)? (No) God forbid.
- **Verse 19:** What? Don't you know that your body is the temple of the Holy Spirit which is in you, which you have been given freely of God, and you are not your own?
- **Verse 20:** For you are bought with a price (the blood of Jesus, shed for you). Therefore glorify God in your (own) body, and in your spirit, which are God's.

Say aloud this faith confession: "My body was not made for sin but for the Lord. My body was not made for sickness but for the Lord. My body is a member of Jesus Christ. My body belongs to Jesus Christ, the Anointed One. Satan cannot make Christ's body sick. Satan, how dare you trespass on God's property. Take your hands off God's property, in Jesus' name. My body is the temple of Jehovah Rapha, the Lord that healeth me. He is in me now, healing me now, for He is the Lord that healeth me. I have been bought with a price, the blood Jesus shed for me. Jesus' blood cleansed me from all sin, and by his stripes my body is healed. I glorify God in my body. I refuse to allow disease in my body, in Jesus' name. You foul disease, take your hands off my body, in Jesus' name. Amen."

- **Galatians 3: 13** – "Christ hath redeemed us from the curse of the law, being made a curse for us: for it is written, Cursed is everyone that hangeth on a tree."

In His death and resurrection Jesus defeated death and broke the curse for us so we can be free and be blessed through Him. Jesus is a mighty blessing. Below is a list of some of the curses of the laws in Deuteronomy 28. Remember, you are redeemed from all the curses. Jesus took them all on himself so that you would not have to have them in your body or in your life. They are not blessings or prosperity. You are entitled to Abraham's blessings, which are listed in verses 1–14 of Deuteronomy 28.

Galatians 3: 13 says, "Christ Jesus redeemed us (believers in Him) from all the curses of the law." Then verse 14 says, "He (Jesus) redeemed us in order that the blessings given to Abraham might come to the Gentiles (people of the world who are not Jews or Israelites) through Christ Jesus, so that by faith we might receive the promise of the Holy Spirit which the Spirit of God made to Abraham." Genesis12:2-3." And I will make of thee a great nation, and I will bless thee and make thy name great;and thou shalt be a blessing. And I will bless them that bless thee and curse them that curse thee and in thee shall all the families of the earth be blessed"

See Genesis 15: 1–19, especially key verses 1–6. Pause, think on it, and then read verses 17–18 again; pause, think. Then read Genesis 17: 1–9.The above verses simply say that God's Spirit made and cut a Hebrew covenant with Abraham and his seed, Jesus, and his descendants (family line) for generations to come and promised it would be an everlasting covenant between God and Abraham's descendants. That's you!

Galatians 3: 26–29 says: If you belong to Christ Jesus then you are Abraham's seed and heirs according to the promise made to you through Abraham's seed, who is Christ. Then you (in Jesus) are heirs, inheritors of all the promises. The key verse is v 29 "And if ye be Christs, then are ye Abraham's seed, and heirs according to the promise."

They are yours, plus everlasting life, plus all the New Testament promises. However, the curses listed in Deuteronomy 28: 15–68 were to come on those, Jews and Gentiles alike, who don't obey the commands given in the Old Testament covenant. No Gentile obeyed God's commands, for all sinned, but the Good News is that *you* inherit all the promises by receiving Christ Jesus as your Lord and Saviour and thereby becoming Abraham's seed. Hallelujah to Jesus! Just ask Jesus to come into your life, and you are brought out of the curses written in Deuteronomy 28: 15–68. These promises, written in Deuteronomy 28:1-14, which verses list all the blessings is b 'racha', empowerment to prosper in all you do. Blessing is b'racha -Hebrew for empowered to prosper, succeed and increase. They are to you and your children because they are your seed (descendants), and you, in Christ, are Abraham's seed! Descendant, you get what Jesus gets, and your kids get it too. Choose to receive it. Come on, readers, do some homework, and read in your Bible what the curses are.

Say this faith confession out loud: "None of these evil curses will come on me because Christ Jesus has redeemed me from the curse of the law. Christ bought me back and freely, as a gift from God, set me free from the curses of the law. I am free, liberated, ransomed. Jesus paid the price for me with the sacrifice of His body and blood given for me. He died for me, took the curse for me, and broke the curse and death in His victorious resurrection. Therefore, I am redeemed from every disease and trouble written in the curse of the Law. This is God's free gift to me. Christ freely gave righteousness to me! I receive it all. Thank you, Jesus."

- **Romans 3: 21–26** – Righteousness comes to everyone who believes in Christ.

To fully understand what righteousness in a person is, you must first totally understand that you are righteous in God's sight when you make Jesus your Lord and Saviour. This calling you righteous is God's idea, God's command, not because you have done or ever could do everything right to please God with your behaviour from past to present or in future. This is a free gift to you who trust that Jesus died in your place. God says when you have accepted Jesus as Lord, He counts you as having right standing with him. Your prayers avail or gain you much favour and blessings (prosperity) from God. James 5: 16 tells you this fact.

So now accept what the Word of God says about you. You have the right to go to God and have all your prayers answered, just the same as all Jesus' prayers were answered because He never sinned. Jesus is the only man ever on this earth to have acted right or righteously before God. Now He gives His rights to you and to all who believe in Him. He took upon Himself all your sin, and by His wounds you are righteous, in right standing with God. You are healed and forgiven of all your sin!

Say out loud: "I am in Christ; therefore righteousness (right standing with God) is freely given to me. Those whom God calls righteous always have their prayers answered with much blessing. My prayer avails me much. Abraham's blessings are mine, through Jesus Christ."

- **Ephesians 4: 27** – Neither give place to the devil (Satan or demons).

Now say this confession aloud: "I refuse to give any place in my life to the devil or demons. Disease and sickness are of the devil. I refuse to give any place to sickness and disease. It is written that if I resist you, then you must flee from me. I belong to God, and I believe His Word."

- **John 14: 12–14** – Verily, verily, I say unto you, he that believes on me, the works that I do shall he do also; and greater works than these shall he do, because I go unto my Father. Whatsoever you shall ask in My name, that will I do, that my Father may be glorified in the Son. If you shall ask anything in My name, I will do it.

Say the faith confession aloud: "There is power in the name of Jesus when I speak it. Jesus is the resurrected healing Lord. In the name of Jesus I command disease to leave (name the person). Jesus said, If I ask anything in His name, He (Jesus) will personally do it for me. Jesus said I have what I believe and say I have. I say in Jesus' name, (name the person) is healed. All glory to Jesus. Amen."

- **John 15: 4–5** – Abide in me and I in you-in Greek the word 'abide' is meno which means to continue to live in Jesus and His Word daily, dwelling in His intimate presence. As the branch cannot bear fruit of (by) itself, except it abide in the vine; no more can you, except you abide in me (Jesus). I am the vine, you are the branches. He that abides in me, and I in him, the same (person) brings forth much fruit, for without me (Jesus) you can do nothing (no work of God).

Say this faith confession aloud: "I am in union with Christ Jesus, the vine. My spirit is in union with Christ the Healer. By faith in Him and His words, I draw out His healing power from Him in me, and it is manifested in my body and those I pray for. I am joined with the healing vine; I'm a fruit-bearing branch, connected totally to the healing vine. I am in union with the healing Christ. I have His life and health in me, flowing through Him, like tree sap, into the branches, giving them life and causing beautiful fruit to grow. I'm a branch. His life is coursing through me, through my veins, my blood. Now I have His life and health in me!

His Word is health and life to all my flesh. I shall bear much fruit, good, long-lasting fruit in abundance. Many people are being released from every kind of sickness and bondage. The words of God which I speak manifest healing now in the physical realm. Amen."

Well, that's a lot of healing words for you! Remember, in order for this medicine of God's Word to penetrate your spirit and be released into your flesh body, you must take the medicine. Hear yourself speak these promises daily; even if you haven't got the time to say them all, say at least some of these confessions daily. Make time to read them and say them daily. If you do, they will work. Speak some of the promises twice a day. If you won't, then it's your choice not to, and you cannot blame God, because you do have the knowledge. Your perishing will not be through a lack of knowledge but through not putting into practice the knowledge you do have of God's Word.

In John 8: 31–32, Jesus said, "If you (yes, you!) continue in My word, you really are My disciples. You will know the truth (the Word or Truth you know), and the truth will set you free." *Free* from illness, *free* from any burden or curse on this planet, *free* from any unwanted things or unwanted situations, poverty, lack, hell, disease, anything in your life. The truth and promises that you know and *do* will free you, and those promises as you *say* and *hear* them will set you *free!*

You cannot eat one meal every week and then eat nothing for the next six days, week after week. If you did, your body would die. You cannot read and hear God's Word for twenty minutes one day a week and pass over it for the next six days, because that way your spirit will be spiritually malnourished and finally starve. God's Word is the food your spirit eats by reading it daily and hearing it daily out of your own mouth or hearing it from anointed men or women who speak it and teach it.

Also, your spirit gains power from communication with God. If you have not yet started to pray in tongues, simply ask God to baptise you in the Holy Spirit now and give you your gift of praying in tongues (in the Spirit). Then as you hear the prayer language in your spirit and mind, say with your own mouth what you hear in your own heart, just let it flow to where you can hear it coming out of your mouth.

- **Luke 11: 9–13,** key verse is verse 13 Your heavenly Father will give the Holy Spirit to those who ask Him.
- **Mark 16:17** which says,"And these signs shall follow them that believe; in my name they shall cast out devils; they shall speak with new tongues.

Ask and receive the Holy Spirit (baptism). Just say, "Jesus, baptise me in the Holy Spirit now. I receive now." He will do it right away (no waiting required). Just ask, believe you receive when you pray (Mark 11: 23–24), and simply say, "Thank You, Father, in Jesus' name. I have tongues now. You gave me the gift when I asked." That's faith in God's promise of Luke 11: 13.

Remember, you want to reap a harvest. Seeds grow into a harvest. Sowing and reaping is a spiritual law, the same as sowing seeds in a field is a law and a necessary step to grow crops. First you sow, plant the seed; then it grows; and you get the harvest. Galatians 6: 7–8 tells you so. Therefore, sow seed into your spirit, and you will reap the Spirit's harvest which is not just eternal life but healings and miracles. The Word (seed) will produce your harvest, i.e., healing and health. Verse 9 says that you will reap a harvest if you continue in your trust in God's Word by believing it and saying it out loud.

Beware, however: Mark 4: 14–15 says the sower sows the Word, but the evil one (Satan) comes in immediately to steal the Word (the seed sown). Don't let the devil steal your harvest of healing by letting some idiot tell you not to bother with this faith stuff, as it does not work. Refuse it immediately! It's the thief, Satan. Don't let him steal the promises, the Word of God, from your heart!

Another ploy can happen when you believe God for healing, but the pain gets worse or the doctor tells you it's not better but worse. That's a sure sign the devils are terrified of you, and they are hoping you will give up and stop saying daily the promises of your healing medicine. Don't fall for it! Just believe and, as Ephesians 6: 13 says, "having done all", stand. Stand determined, rigid against this attack. Resist the devil and his thoughts and attacks, and he will flee from you (James 4: 7). Don't let him wear you down. Remember, faith comes by hearing and hearing by God's Word. Romans 10:17 says so.

If you are thinking on the promises, as you hear them, you cannot think about being sick or listening to the devil's bad news or someone he sends to tell you bad news. You can't think about two things at the same time. Occupy your mind with God's Word. Faith and trust will rise up in you, leading to health. Keep on speaking the Word for as long as it takes. It won't take long if you make a quality decision to simply continue to believe God and do what you know to do. Say, "Devil, I believe God's Word. It's my covenant, and I refuse to believe any bad news. I choose instead to continue taking the medicine, and my medicine will work."

Important: Once you feel healed, another ploy of Satan is to get you to give up your new-found health after some time. Suppose you are feeling pain or a symptom of the sickness you were healed from. If this happens, immediately say to the part of your body being attacked, "Stay whole, stay healed. Pain, symbol of sickness, leave me now. I received my healing, and I resist you, Satan! You are not putting that old sickness or problem back into me." James 4: 7 says. "Resist the devil, and he will flee from you." So resist any pain or symptoms that return and take heart. Resist him, and keep on saying the promises daily. Even when you believe you're healed, keep on daily saying some promises. This will keep all illness from you and will prevent illnesses, because you are now using the Word promises as a prevention to keep all sickness off you. So if any pain or symptom returns after you feel healed, don't panic. Resist them by speaking to them saying, "Pain, leave me now."

Now you know the two weapons the devil always uses: (1) bad news by way of a thought or some person telling you it won't work; and (2) a pain or symptom recurring after you have actually started to feel better. Don't go by your feelings; go by what the Word says. There is no faith in feelings; that's where the devil operates, in feelings. "Don't you feel bad? Yes, you do. What's the use of trying? You know you feel sick." Blah, blah. If this happens, it's just old thick-head Satan. Resist him! It's the same old trick. It's all he has. He has no new tricks.

By your words you will stand or fall. Mark 11: 23 tells you clearly that Jesus said, "You shall have what you say." You are the prophets of your own life. Forewarned is forearmed. You are warned before it happens. Praise God, you know what to expect, and you know how to stop every attack of Satan and sickness. Revelation 12: 11 says it's by the blood of

Jesus and using the name of Jesus that we prevail. For this knowledge, praise Him, praise Jesus, who shows you how to overcome Satan.

I'm like you, simply an instrument of God, a servant passing on to you what God has taught me. Believe me, I have been through all these attacks, and I have proved for myself that God's Word works when I put it to work. Patience and faith are the power twins you must have and use. Imitate those people who through using their faith and patience inherit (receive into their life) what God has promised.

Here is an example. A man has ten thousand pounds in his bank account, put there by his grandfather as a gift. It was his inheritance. He knows this because he received a letter from his grandfather's lawyer saying that, before he died, he left instructions to deposit that amount directly into his bank account. If you are poor and have never even seen a hundred pounds, never mind ten thousand, and you never even knew your grandfather had such a sum for you, you would be surprised. You now have to believe the lawyer's letter – believe his word. If you believe the letter and the Will, you go to the bank, take your cheque book to the counter clerk, sign the cheque, and ask the clerk for the cash. You have to act, do something about the news you just received and believed.

Many Christians today don't believe they have a list of inheritance promises from God, so they continue to live under the curses of the Law, such as illness, poverty, and depression. This is even though they are redeemed from them by the blood of Jesus and it's their inheritance to have health, peace, and financial prosperity if only they would believe God's promises (the lawyer's letter) and *act* on the promises. They need to say to God, "Praise You, Father (the grandfather). I receive now my inheritance. Healing, health, peace, joy, and financial prosperity (the bank balance), and I'm saying it's mine. I receive it. I expect it earnestly to be manifested in my body now (in health and wholeness)." That is the *act* (walking into the bank, signing the cheque, handing it in, and getting the cash). The *act* in God's Word is saying to God, "Yes, I believe. I receive now my inheritance", and then just watching it come into your hands. That's *faith* in what God said is yours.

Now what about patience? In Hebrews 6: 12, God's Word speaks on patience and faith, saying that those who were prepared to wait for the promise received their inheritance. Patience is sometimes required when a person is waiting for something promised by God or even by people. Suppose a grandfather leaves you money in his Will, but another of his grandchildren decides to contest or oppose the Will and says, "I'm taking this case to court, as I believe I should have the money. It's not fair that you should get it, and I have a legal right to contest you, even though the money is in your name on the Will." Legally, you will not get the money right away. It will be delayed until the judge hears evidence from both you and the contesting grandchild. The case may take a year or even two years to end. The judge, after reading the Will and seeing your name in the Will, written in your grandfather's handwriting, will award the money to you. Quite rightly so. It's justice. You need patience to wait for the case of your relative's objection to be heard, judged, and concluded, in order to receive the promise from your grandfather.

Now this is important: what if you got fed up waiting for the case to start? Say the court said the judge will hear your case in twelve months' time, and you said, "I can't be bothered to wait twelve months and then maybe another few months for the final decision. So I'm not going to court." You would not get the money until you decided to fight for it legally in the judge's presence. If you decided never to contest it, you would never receive the money. It would remain in the court's custody in their account. Well, you have a contender (the devil) for your promise (God's Word, the promise of healing to you), and unless you take the time to let the judge (Jesus) rule in your favour that the promise is yours and fight off the contender (the devil) by continuing daily to confess your rights in Jesus, you will not receive the promise. You must tell the devil, "God has promised me healing in my covenant, and Jesus has ruled it's mine. I will keep on patiently saying aloud and reading aloud the healing promises. I know faith comes by hearing and hearing by God's word. No one can receive any promise from God except by faith; nor can anyone please God except by faith, believing God. So I will patiently, daily expect my wholeness even if it takes three months or six months or two years. I believe God's Word. You can contest my healing, devil, but the judge, Jesus, has already pronounced that 'by His wounds, I am healed'. Matthew 8: 16–17 says so. I will be patient. and I will have faith, and therefore, as Hebrews 6: 12 says, I will receive all my inheritance, of which healing is a part (Psalm 103: 3 says so), one of God's benefits among Abraham's blessings which, as God promised to Abraham and his Seed, Jesus, will come upon me. I'm a Gentile, a non-Jew, but through Christ Jesus healing is a part of the covenant blessings, and Galatians 3: 13–14 says so. So I'm not giving up, I am going to contest you, devil. I believe God's promises. He's my dad, *Abba*, Father, and He cannot lie. You can and do, devil. The Bible, God's Word, says you are and were a liar from the beginning, the father of lies. John 8: 44 says so. I will wait. I will be patient, and therefore I will receive, I will inherit all that God has promised. James 4: 7, God's Word, also says that if I resist you and your lies, you will flee from me."

Now it's up to you. Choose to be free, please, in Jesus' name. I pray Jesus will open your heart and mind to know and do and continue to do what you know you should do. *Amen.*

Beloved readers, as 3John 1:2 says, I pray and hope that above all things you prosper (lack no good thing in life) and be in health (no illness) even as your soul (mind) prospers (receives more knowledge of what God has promised you) in His covenant word. Amen.

Faith and Confession = Victory.

CHAPTER 5

AVOID THE SUFFERING CAUSED THROUGH POVERTY

An introduction

We are going to deal more specifically with financial prosperity in chapter 6, including what God said about money, lands, goods, etc., and what God said He would give to those who believe in Him, who belong to Jesus, and who give as God instructs. God still wants His followers to tithe (give back to God 10 per cent of their income) and give offerings freely to the Lord and His work over and above the tithe. However, first you must know deep in your spirit and mind what God in His Word has promised about these things.

Never let anyone convince you to give up your God-promised harvests of blessings: financial, material, social, lands, houses, goods, etc. Many scholars and theologians misinterpret God's Word, as do many religious Christians. They don't believe God wants you to have money and things to enjoy. There are many who say God does not want us to have anything to do with riches or money, and most of them can quote a few Scriptures that seemingly back up their view that God wants us poor.

The trouble with most of these types of people, and I have met many, is this: they usually have two cars, a holiday home or caravan, a big house, and nice clothes; they eat the best food and have at least one holiday each year for their whole family. Even vicars do this! That's okay with me and God, but they are the religious ones who say, "Well, you know, too much is not good for people, and it will probably ruin them, break up their marriage, etc., through wild living, or they will forget about God altogether." Yet it's okay in their minds for them to have the best.

Well, if it's good for them, it's good for us. What's good for the goose is good for the gander. Watch out, because they don't practice what they preach. True followers of Jesus love to give and live to give, but you can't give if you don't have. If these people who preach that lack (just enough) or poverty is from God do believe they are right, then why don't they get rid of all their stuff and live with nothing but bare necessities for themselves and their families? It's because they don't really believe it. For themselves it's okay to have abundance, but not for you. Who are they to judge who should have and who should not have? Praise God, they are not our judge; Jesus is.

Let's find out exactly what God says about His will concerning money, lands, and goods. Then when you do know, you must hang on to what you know and believe it. God says in Hebrews 11: 6 that you must (NIV): "Without faith (in God and what He says) it is impossible to please God, because anyone who comes to Him must believe that He exists and that He rewards those who earnestly seek him." Believe God rewards all who diligently seek to know Him and know His Word, what it really means. Do you see it? I pray you will. If you've no faith in what God says and promises, it causes Him to respond, "You don't please Me; it's impossible until you decide to believe in Me and My promises, believe I exist, that I'm alive and here, and accept that I want with all my heart to reward you who seek to know Me and My will, which is My Word." If you don't or won't, then it's not God's fault that you never receive rewards in your life. Now please patiently read Chapter 5 in order to understand and accept Chapter 6.

Question: Does God (Yahweh – Jesus) want his people to prosper, financially, materially, and socially and prosper in health, mind, and spirit? By explanation, God's name is Yahweh; in Hebrew YHWH. You pronounce this YUD HEI VAV HEI and in English you say, Yud Hay Vav Hay. These are the four Hebrew letters for God's name. Here is the reason: *Jesus* is our Savour's name in Greek, but His name in Hebrew is Yeshua, which means Yahweh's Saviour. Christ, which is a Greek word, in Hebrew is Messiah which means Yahweh's anointed King. Conclusion: Jesus is Yahweh; Yahweh is God, and God is an English name.

Answer: Simply, yes. The Bible, God's Word says yes. John 1:1-3 says "In the beginning was the Word, and the Word was with God, and the Word was God. The same was in the beginning with God. All things were made by Him and without Him was not anything made that was made. Verse 10-15 explains this clearly.

Question: Why are so many Christians not prospering?

Answer: God's people are perishing through a lack of knowledge of God's Word, not knowing what's rightfully theirs (their inheritance). These people have different reasons for not believing that God wants them blessed and prosperous. The exact truth is that if they would do what the Word says to do and believe that God will reward, bless, and prosper them, prosperity would come to them now and enable them to help others and give to God's work here on earth. Then they could enjoy what's left for themselves and their families or friends, without guilt and with joy.

Let's look at what God says from His Word, and then we can see for ourselves – not what men and women say about prosperity but what God himself says about it. Let's look at 3 John 2, which says this, "Brothers (fellow believers in Jesus), I desire above all things that you prosper (lack no good thing) and be in health even as your soul and mind prosper." Now we know that God's Word says that all Scripture in the Bible is inspired by God (comes from God's mouth) and is written down for us all to read. Second Timothy 3: 16 says so: God-breathed!

Faith (trust in God's Word) never allows your destiny to be settled by chance. Once you know what's yours and you follow the instructions, it won't be long before you receive and enjoy what's yours, promised by God to you in his covenant agreement, sealed in the blood of Jesus. This is what 3 John 2 was talking about when God said (through John), "even as your soul (mind) prospers" (that is, increases in knowledge of God's Word). Now you know, you can decide whether or not to put into practice in your life what you know you should do. Do you see it? Yes, I pray you will.

Now let's look at various promises on prosperity and where they are found in the Bible. Remember, God's promises have a condition on each of them. God gives instruction for you to do something, and then He promises that He will accomplish something for you. You have

God's Word that His commands are never too hard for you to carry out. Remember, you always have the choice of the blessing or the curse. If you are smart you will do what God wants and receive the great blessings with material and financial rewards. There are many, many promises that say God wants you well in body, having a long life on earth, and also that God wants you to have abundance of finances and material things. This is not popular with the traditions of the Christian churches and denominations today, but it's the exact truth, and God, as the Scriptures say, is full of mercy and is good. God rewards those people who diligently, loyally believe in Him and do His will, which is His Word. So if you want to know for sure what God's will is regarding money and material goods for his people, you have to go to His word.

Any other teaching from anyone, whether Christian or non-Christian, is what Jesus calls the "traditions of men" – errors or lies taught by men or women wanting to persuade you that God wants you poor or not to have too much, especially that you can't be rich in goods or money, because it's heresy or ungodly. That statement is a lie and not God's Word. God didn't say it.

They say God wants you in lack, because poverty humbles you and keeps you from being proud. It's a lie of the devil in order for you to agree with human traditions. On the contrary, they are dulling the word of God with their traditions. Read Colossians 2: 8, and do not let men take you captive with deception. Also, read Matthew 15: 1–9, and don't be deceived, The key verse here is verse 6. The devil knows he can't keep you in lack or poverty – he does not have the power or authority – so he endeavours to deceive you into saying and believing you will never be rich or prosperous. He knows you will get what you say because God Himself said so. Mark 11:24, Matthew 21:22 and Luke 17:6 all say so.

In order to be blessed you must say what the Word of God says about you. Then and only then will you have it, see it, and be able to hold, own, and use the money and material goods He provides in order to effectively serve Him. Give where God directs and blesses; help the poor, the needy, and the homeless because you now have more than enough, much more than enough, and you can give much more away. Do you see it? I pray you will. That's the way God in Jesus sees it. Then, after you have given, you will always have abundantly more left over for yourself, family, and friends. This leftover excess abundance is your reward.

You must believe what God alone has promised you concerning prosperity and say, "Yes, Lord, I joyfully receive it, because You will it for me, and I believe and accept what You say, which is written in my Bible. It is my copy of my covenant rights." If anyone tells you that no, God does not want you prosperous, just smile and pray for them to know what you know and peacefully walk away – or, if they are willing to listen to you, explain prosperity to them as God leads you! It was never God's will for any of the curses or failure to come on His people or anyone else in this world!

The Bible is truth. Everything in the Bible is truthfully stated, but not everything in the Bible is a statement of truth. Please read that again.

The definition of exact truth is always what God says about something and has it written down in your Bible. For example, "Thus says the Lord" or "God said" or"God spoke" or "God promised" or "Jesus said" or "Jesus promised" this or that. These are the things which are written down, what God Himself said or promised. Anything anyone else says, if God did not say it, is just an opinion, uttered out of lack of knowledge or the desire to deceive. The Bible records many instances where things went wrong, very wrong, and people blamed God. In order to understand that God wants all people to prosper in every area of life, we have to look at a few examples of those who were in error when they said, "It is God's will for these bad things to happen." We need to reiterate that *the Bible is truth. Everything in the Bible is truthfully stated, but not everything in the Bible is a statement of truth.* Please read and digest.

A simple example of something truthfully stated and truthfully written down, which is an error or a lie, is this. A man has a secretary. Imagine the man has never seen or heard of a dog. The only information he has about a dog is what other people have told him. These people have never actually seen a dog either. He says to his secretary, "Write this down on paper, as I honestly believe this. A dog is big, with two heads and six legs." His secretary writes down exactly what the man says, that a dog is big and has two heads and six legs. This is a lie or an error. Yet the man truly believes it, and his secretary wrote it down exactly as she was instructed. So therefore it is truthfully stated, but it is not a statement of truth. The exact truth is that a dog has one head and four legs and can be big, small, or medium in size. Okay? Do you see it?

There are quite a few instances in the Bible like this. God did not say it; people based their statements on a lack of knowledge or on misinformation, or they knowingly lied in order to keep the truth from someone or everyone! Read your Bible daily, and pray and ask God, by His Holy Spirit, to show you exactly what He said and to make known to you the errors from people who lack knowledge. It works for me and will for anyone who will spend time studying and praying for revealed knowledge.

The definition of revealed knowledge is this: knowledge revealed by the Holy Spirit directly to your spirit in order for you to understand something exactly as God intended. The Holy Spirit *must* be involved, as this is His job! It's to reveal God's truth to your heart and your spirit about what you are reading in the Bible. All you have to do is say, "Lord Jesus, reveal to me through your Holy Spirit the exact truth of what I am reading in my Bible. Show me, help me to understand." Do this, and God will do His part and show you the truth of His promises and how to receive them! Be patient, wait till you hear God.

The reason God has allowed the errors and lies that people have done and said to be recorded in the Bible is to give you real-life examples of what not to do, what not to say, and what not to believe. It's so that you will know for certain what not to do and are confident of what you should do. God has allowed some of these truthfully stated but erroneous assertions to be recorded so we do not unnecessarily have to suffer the same problems as those we are reading about – those who suffered needlessly through their lack of knowledge. It's for us who are "born again" by God's Spirit and who diligently study God's Word, daily asking Him to explain to us exactly what His Word means, so we can understand and prosper.

Question: What has this to do with money or material prosperity or avoiding lack or poverty?

Answer: Everything. If you don't know with certainty that God wants you to have an abundance of every good thing, then you will suffer unnecessarily and blame God. The only way to avoid being deceived by false teachers is for you personally to daily spend quality time reading the Word. Each day ask Jesus to reveal to you the exact truth of His Word, His promises on prosperity that He himself paid for and sealed by His blood. You have a covenant right to be blessed, to be prospered financially, because God Himself said so.

Let's take a quick look at some of God's people who suffered needlessly and blamed God for their mistaken beliefs, believing that terrible things had come from Him. Let's look first at Abraham. Yes, Abraham! He made quite a few mistakes, and so did Abraham's, wife Sarai – or Sarah, as most people know her. I assume all people, even non-Christians, know that God Himself commanded His people, all people, *"Thou shalt not lie."* It's one of the Ten Commandments. Now Abraham and Sarah knew God did not want them to lie! They knew God wanted them to trust Him to keep His promises to them, to give them a child from Abraham's sperm through Sarah's barren womb. They still made excuses and lied, and they would not exercise faith or trust in God, who had said they would have a child of your own (not adopted). They both even laughed in God's presence when He promised them a child. Abraham and Sarah both knew what God had promised them: that if they kept His commands all would go well for them, they would always be blessed, prospered, and protected. However, if they did not keep His Word, things would go wrong. Lying and not believing, not having faith in what God said to them and promised them, violated their part of the covenant (Gen. 17: 15–19). God in His mercy still got them out of their troubles (into which they had got themselves!). Praise God. But things did go wrong.

Deuteronomy 11: 26–28 tells of the blessings for obeying God and curses (problems) for disobeying. Abraham lied to the Egyptian officials of Pharaoh by telling them that Sarah was his sister, not his wife. They took Sarah to the Pharaoh's harem to be one of his concubines! Abraham did this to save his own life, because he believed Pharaoh's officials would kill him and take Sarah by force if he told them she was his wife. Fear! See Genesis 12: 10–13 for this account. Things went wrong, very wrong! When God promised Abraham and Sarah a child, they didn't believe Him and Abraham laughed as recorded in Genesis 17: 17 "and said in his heart, "shall a child be born to a man who is a hundred years old?"" In Genesis 15: 2, Abraham bemoans his situation, asking, "What can you give us, God, seeing we go childless?"

Question: Who said God couldn't give them a child? Who spoke lies? Who laughed at what God said?

Answer: Two people, Abraham and Sarah did. It's not God's Word. Did God tell them to lie? No! Did God say, "Don't trust Me to protect you against a King or Pharaoh because they are too powerful for Me to handle"? No. Yet it's recorded in the Bible. It's exactly what happened. It's the truth but it's not what God said. Do see the difference? Beware the traditions of men.

God promised to Abraham's child (and descendants) the land of Canaan. See Genesis 12: 7. Read it for yourself. Let's take a look at Sarah, Abraham's wife, and read Genesis 18: 9–15. God told Abraham that Sarah would have a child when she was ninety years old. Sarah had been barren, unable to have a child all her life. She was close by and heard with her own ears what God said, that she, from her womb, would have a child from Abraham, by his sperm. Sarah laughed, and God heard her. Now Sarah was afraid, so she lied to God, saying she hadn't laughed at what He'd promised to Abraham. God said, "Yes! You did laugh." God had the last word, not Sarah! God always has the first and last word in everything. Be thankful for this truth. The point is, God wanted to prosper Sarah and Abraham with a son that Sarah had deeply desired. It was all truthfully described, written down in the Bible, but the only accurately reported truth in the above chapter and verses was what God said.

Question: So does the Bible instruct us to lie as Sarah and Abraham did?

Answer: No! Emphatically no! And yes, I know that the law of Moses was not in force at that time. Abraham was under God's grace, but he and Sarah knew what was right and what was wrong. Abraham chose to save his own skin at Sarah's expense, because of his fear.

Question: Does the Bible instruct us to laugh at God's commands and promises and say out loud (even in churches), "God can't or won't do this for us today. It's too hard for us to believe what God has written and promised to us in Christ"?

Answer: No! Emphatically, no!

Question: Why did God allow these truthful, accurate reports of Abraham and Sarah's unbelief, mockery, and lies to be recorded?

Answer: So that we don't make the same mistakes. We can say to God, "Yes, Lord, I believe you will do exactly for me as you said. I fully expect it to come to me! I am praising You now, because as Mark 11: 23–24 says, I have what I say." Learn to read the Bible in a thoughtful, Holy

Spirit–revealed way! Always pray first, asking God to reveal to you exactly what He Himself intends for you to fully understand. Now don't worry! We're still on the point of prosperity and the fact that God wants you prosperous. Don't worry!

Abraham and Sarah did eventually change, and they were forgiven by God. When Abraham at last believed God, a child named Isaac from Abraham's sperm was born from Sarah's formerly dead, barren womb, just as God said would happen. Yes, God forgives our weakness, unbelief, and disobedience (just confess them), but He expects us, just like Abraham, to ultimately trust Him to do what He promised us! That's why we must find out for ourselves what the Bible, our covenant, God's Word, says, by spending time reading, studying, and learning to ask God (in Jesus' name) to reveal to us the exact truth of what we are reading.

Genesis 18: 14 says, "Is anything too hard for Yahweh God?" "I say, just like You, God, nothing is too hard for You, and according to Hebrews 6: 12, I'm going to have faith in what You said. I'm going to be patient, and through faith and patience I will receive my inheritance rights, all that I'm believing You for." Then, just as God said to Abraham in Genesis 15: 6, "I credit this to you as righteousness because you have believed what I, God, have promised", He will also say to you, "Well done, you good and faithful son or daughter, you're a good servant as well as my son or daughter!"

Check out Luke 8: 11–15 and especially key verse 15; read all of it. Hear the Word, believe it, retain it in your heart by being patient, and produce a crop harvest. Yes, the seed in Luke 8: 11 is the Word, and believing the Word seed produces your financial crop, your harvest, or whatever you're believing God for that's promised by Him in His Word, *the Bible*.

Let's have one more example of a written story in the Bible where disaster struck a certain man, Job! Job lived around 1845 BC. The time the book of Job was written was probably between 1843 BC and 1703 BC, but it may have been written after this time. The period of Job's testing was nine months, according to some Bible scholars, and after this Job received twice as much back from God as he had lost.

Remember, Job lived a long time before Luke (the disciple of Jesus) who wrote down the things that Jesus did and said. Read Luke 1: 1–4, where he says, "I, Luke, have carefully investigated everything Jesus did and said from the beginning. It seemed good to me to write down an orderly account for you so that you may know the certainty of the things you have been taught."

Question: Could Job open his Bible and read about the New Covenant or look up his list of covenant rights? Could Job read in Luke's gospel about his authority over the devil and demons and bind them and cast them out in Jesus' name? Could Job open up any of the Gospels or the New Testament letters and find out that God gives and the devil steals, takes away, kills, destroys, and scatters God's lambs (people) like a wolf? Could Job open the book of Luke and find it written that there was an enemy called the devil, Satan?

Answer: No

Question: Why?

Answer: The gospel of Luke had not yet been written (neither had the rest of New Testament) explaining all things about God and the devil. Who was giving? It was God. Who was taking away? It was Satan. Job didn't know then that there is a heaven reserved for people made right through faith in Jesus' blood sacrifice; then God sees them not only as righteous but in His sight, good. To God the definition of *good* is that "you have no sin counted against you". Neither did Job know that there was a hell (prison) reserved for the devil and his angels (demons). No, Job lived long before (1845 BC) God had time legally to send Jesus and to reveal all truth about what God promised and commanded.

Job was perishing through a lack of knowledge of God's Word! Before Jesus, humanity had no authority over Satan; instead, Satan had authority over people until Jesus came 1845 years later, took authority back from Satan, and gave it to us believers in Christ. Job had no authority over Satan and could not, therefore, bind him or stop him from destroying his goods or his children and livestock (Author's note) Job got exactly what he said: "All these things I feared have come upon me." Remember Luke 8: 11–15, which explains that if you hear God's Word (exactly what God said and had written down), believe it, and retain it in your heart and mind, then the word is like a seed which grows and produces a harvest in your life, a good crop of good things.

Question: Could Job know that the promises in the Word of God are like seeds and that the seed will always grow into a harvest (a fruit) exactly like the seed, good or badIn Mark 11:23-24 Jesus said you shall have what you ask God for if you believe in your heart, but most importantly, you shall have what you say

Answer: No, emphatically, no! It had not yet been written. Job thought there was only one super being, God, Yahweh, the Creator of all things. He was right about this, but Job had no knowledge of evil fallen angels on earth, powerful enemies who were enemies of God and enemies of Job and his family. He didn't know Satan sought to destroy them, to steal his great wealth of lands, livestock, and financial prosperity. Job was a very rich man! All Scripture is inspired and true, written down by the prompting of the Holy Spirit. See 2 Timothy 3: 16, where we're told that the Word is God-breathed. The Bible was intended to be written down so we could be taught, corrected, trained in righteousness, to do things God's way. It was to teach what God said and what He didn't say. It was also for rebuking us, telling us off (as sometimes we need telling off), to be sharply told (by God's Word), stop this or that, it's wrong. Jesus said in Matthew 6: 25–33, "seek first the kingdom of God (his way of doing things), and all these things (material goods and wealth), which the non-believers run after, shall be given unto you," without you chasing them, spending all your time purchasing them by working all the hours God sends. Now we can be confident that Job's story is exact truth. If you read Job 7: 18–21, you will see that today we can find out exactly who it was who did those terrible things to Job simply by reading the account in the book of Job! We can find out exactly who did what and why Job lost everything. God later restored it all, twice over. See Job 42: 10–16, especially key verse 10: Job did not, could not at the time of his suffering, have known for sure who was behind his troubles. It was Satan, but Job did not even know Satan existed, let alone that he was a rebellious (former) archangel of God (see Job 1: 6–7). As a result, Job blamed God for lots of things and made foolish statements as for example in Job 1: 21, "The Lord God gives and the Lord God then takes it away."

Question: Who did these things to Job's family and servants?

Answer: See Job 2: 4–10, especially key verse 7. Satan afflicted Job with painful sores from head to foot all over his body – a horrible disease. God did not do it!

Question: If God did not do it, then why did God (on the face of it) allow Satan to attack and test Job? Why didn't God just stop Satan from attacking Job and his family?

Answer: God had no right to stop Satan!

Question: Did God have the power to stop Satan?

Answer: Yes, much more power than Satan. God's power is almighty, absolute.

Question: Why didn't God use His greater power to intervene and stop Satan from attacking Job and his family? Why didn't God send His angels to protect Job; that is one of the tasks given to a guardian angel?

Answer: God had no legal right to stop Satan or use an angel to stop Satan!

Question: Why did God have no legal right to stop Satan?

Answer: God can only do what His Word says! Because God's first man, Adam, gave all his authority over planet earth to Lucifer, who became Satan, then Satan owned all the kingdoms of men and women on earth. Read Genesis 3:1-17 which speaks of the deception and fall of man; also read Luke 4:5-6 which describes Satan's failed attempt to get Jesus to worship him. Because Satan lost to Jesus, Jesus in His death and resurrection legally took back all Satan's authority and power and disarmed him totally. He is a defeated foe. God can only do what He said He would do or promised. We read in James 1: 6–8 that the person who doubts God is like a wave of the sea, blown and tossed one way then the other by the wind. That man who doubts should not think he will receive anything from the Lord because he is a double-minded man, unstable in all he does.

Question: Why didn't Job receive God's protection for his family, his goods, his livestock, his health, etc., when God's will was for his protection?

Answer (part 1): The only protection from Satan that Job had or anybody has is the shield of faith. Ephesians 6: 16 tells us that when our shield of faith is down, on the floor rather than held in front of us, then and only then are Satan and demons able to devour us. See 1 Peter 5: 8, which says that Satan is as a roaring lion, seeking someone weak in faith to devour. Notice too that Job, according to the Bible, was very righteous, good, generous (to the poor), and religious, a God-fearing man. Yet none of these good points was sufficient to cause God to protect him or his family. Job only understood after God had revealed to him that he could choose life or death, blessings or cursing. See Deuteronomy 30: 19.

Answer (part 2): Job did not have what we have today, knowledge from God's Word telling us we must have faith in God's promises and that those promises must be received through faith or trust in what God has already sworn in His Word. Proverbs 18: 21 says, "Life and death is in the power of the tongue," in what a person believes and chooses to say about his life. Can you see it? Job lacked both faith in what God said and the knowledge that life or death, blessing or cursing was his choice. He also lacked the knowledge that Satan, not God, was responsible for his family's destruction and his riches being stolen. Satan was responsible for his sickness (dreadful life-threatening illness), his depression (Job wanted to die) and the misery that drove him to curse the day he was born (Job 3: 1–3). At this time Job had no knowledge of life and death being in the power of his tongue because as yet the book of Proverbs (including Prov. 18: 21) had not been written. He was never suicidal through all the evils that befell him and his house (about nine months), yet Job thought it was God! Check out Job 1: 21 and 6: 4. Then read Job 5: 17–18. Here, Eliphaz says God was correcting Job and disciplining him (with all the evils), wounding him and injuring him! Then Eliphaz adds insult to injury and says, "After He has injured you, He will heal you!"

Question: How did God heal all his dead children if Eliphaz was right?

Answer: All Job's children, killed by Satan, remained stone dead, and Job's children – supposedly disciplined and injured by God – remained dead.

Question: If Eliphaz was right, what did Job's children learn through God (supposedly) killing them?

Answer: Nothing at all; they were dead. Do you see it? It was not God but Satan! The book of Job says so; Eliphaz was wrong. So where do we look in God's Word to prove Job had no faith in what God said and verify that all the bad things that had happened to Job were because of what Job had said? All his married life, after his children were born, Job actually feared, really feared that one day all those evils would come upon his children and that all his riches and farm animals would be lost. Job feared his children were doing terrible things behind his back and that one day God would punish them. Job 8: 4, 1: 5, and 3: 25 affirm this. (Don't worry, I'm still on the prosperity message. Be patient, and please read on. You will see why as the chapter unfolds.)

Job's story ends fantastically and happy ever after, thanks to God explaining things to him, but only when Job realised and said in Job 42: 3, "Therefore I have spoken, uttered things I did not understand" – things like Satan, demons, spirits, and angels, about enormous creatures, about "things too wonderful for me, which I did not understand." In 38 1–7, God said to Job, "You speak of my counsel, what I really do, without true knowledge of exactly who is your problem. You, Job, were not there at the beginning of this planet earth to see it being made."

Verse 7 is the key verse. This is revelation to Job and to us, that "while the morning stars sang together," all the angels (including Lucifer) and his followers – Lucifer, the Angel of Light now renamed Satan or Enemy and Accuser by God – " shouted for joy" at the wonderful sight of a planet (earth) being created in space before their eyes. Satan was a cherub angel. Now Job knew there were other mighty beings called angels who existed with God, before he (Job) was born! Angels are not as powerful as God (Yahweh, Jehovah) but nevertheless mighty enough to cause Job and his family trouble, sickness, and death. In the beginning of our earth Lucifer and all the other angels were servants of God. Later, Satan and approximately one third of the angels rebelled against God. They then became demons, enemies of God. We read about this in an earlier chapter of this book (chapter 3). That is one of the main reasons Job said in 42: 1–6, with attention to key verse 3, "Surely I spoke of things I did not understand." Job and his three mates said, "The Lord gives and the Lord then takes away what he gives in order to punish innocent men." Job now knew it was not God, and at last, hallelujah, Job was what? Trusting God again; he had peace.

Question: Why did Job now have faith again that God would do him good?

Answer: Because now he no longer had confused thinking. He knew for certain it was not God taking away. He knew for certain there were other heavenly beings, angels, some good, God's servants, and some bad former angels, now rebels, namely Satan and his demon mob. Once the lack of knowledge and wisdom was filled, the confusion went, the fear went, and faith or trust in God and what God said and promised came in place of fear. Read Job 42 :10-17 and you will see that God restored to Job double for all he lost and added another 140 years to his life to recompense him for Satan's attacks.

Faith activates God. Fear activates Satan. Read Proverbs 18: 21: "Life and death is in the power of your tongue." Because you think fearful things, you will say them aloud. Then Satan hears your confession and brings to pass what you say, as in Mark 11: 23–24. Jesus said you are the prophet of your own life; you shall have whatsoever you both believe and say. It's up to you. Watch your tongue! Don't say bad things are going to happen to you. Never say God will not help you! He will, if you simply say, "Jesus, I'm sorry. Forgive me. I repent. I receive Your mercy and forgiveness. Help me watch what I say." Then say aloud, "In Jesus' name, I command a harvest now." Don't worry about the bad things you said (that's from Satan). Trust God to forgive you, and don't look back. Start saying and thinking good things will come from God, from Jesus Himself, towards you and your family. Resist Satan and say, "In Jesus' name, take your hands off my health, my finances, my children, in fact, everything" and then submit yourself to God. Tell God that you trust Him to do all He says, all He promises to do for you, your children, wife, and friends, and for anyone you pray for.

Do all you can to keep God's ways and commands. If like Job, you sometimes fail or do wrong, go to God and say sorry, confess what you did! Run to Him, not away from Him. First John 1: 9 tells us that "God is just and faithful to forgive us of our sins and to cleanse us of all unrighteousness." Then go free, knowing God will bless you and your children. Throw your guilt away. Believe what God said in 1 John 1: 9. That's God's promise to you. Don't make Job's mistake, saying, "All these things I have feared have come upon me." No, resist Satan, and submit to God's Word. Say, "Devil, I know it's you. I know I'll be forgiven in Jesus. I know my God will deliver me from you. I know He will heal me and prosper me, in mind and money and goods and body. When He does, I will use lots of the money and things to give to my God and His people to bring His kingdom to earth and destroy yours."

Go free, my brothers and sisters; drink in this message! Do you see it? It's pure Bible truth, discerned and interpreted by the Holy Spirit. Like

Jesus said in Mark 11: 23–24, you have what you believe and say. Satan has to obey God when God commands him to do something which is covenant (legal) related. According to God's promises, when you have believed God, that is, trusted Him, He will do exactly all you trust Him to do for you and yours, simply because God said He would, and He cannot lie, as Numbers 23: 19 and Proverbs 30: 5 verify. The Word is flawless. Once He says He will, He does. He cannot and does not change His commands or promises; they are forever!

The Bible says of Jesus in Hebrews 13: 8 that He is *the same yesterday, today and forever!* Jesus kept His Word, His promises, yesterday. Jesus keeps His Word, His promises, today. And Jesus will keep His Word, His promises, forever. Jesus (God) is the same, past, present, future, yesterday, today, and tomorrow. He healed yesterday, in the past, and as He does not change, He still heals today, in the present, and will always heal tomorrow, in the future. So if anyone says, "Jesus healed two thousand years ago, but God's changed His mind, and He does not heal now", that's a lie or deception. You who know the promises, God's Word, you can with all certainty say "*No!* He cannot change because it's written, and I know I can trust the words God spoke to me and all his children in Christ." It's the same with all God's promises, prosperity promises included. Psalm 89:34 says that God will not break His covenant nor alter the thing that has gone forth out of His mouth saith Yahweh.

Question: Who said, "I tell you the truth, if anyone gives for my sake and the gospel's (gives money or goods, lands, homes, buildings, etc.), I promise they will receive back, now in this age (on earth), a hundred times more or at least many more times than what they gave"? See Mark 10: 27–30 and Luke 18: 27–30.

Answer: Jesus.

Question: Does this hundredfold promise, to anyone who gives for His sake and the gospel's, change because it's the year 2015 or beyond?

Answer: No, no! Because Jesus and His Word are the same yesterday, today, and tomorrow. He cannot change. He cannot change His Word. It's written. It is part of the blood covenant. The command is "If anyone gives for my sake and the gospel's, then I promise you will receive one hundred times as much as you gave, now, in this age (on earth now, lands, homes, goods)." Harvest is progressive and in proportion to your faith.

Jesus said that anyone who gives for His sake and the gospel's shall receive on earth now in this age thirty or sixty or a hundredfold back. So there are variations in the harvest you receive from God. It's your choice. You can have what you say. If you say God will give thirty-fold of what you say, you will receive thirty-fold; if you say sixty-fold or a hundredfold, you will receive according to your faith. You get God's best. If you say, "I will receive five times as much", you will get five times as much. You sow the seed, and the amount of the harvest is what you believe and say. The good news is that you will always receive a generous multiplication on your giving to God.

As an example, let's imagine you have five acres of land, and you give it to a ministry that wants to build a stadium that holds 50,000 people. The purpose of the building is to preach God's Word, the Gospel of Jesus. Jesus has promised you five hundred acres – yes, five hundred acres of land back! The five acres you gave times a hundred equals five hundred acres. How much could you sell the five hundred acres for? Millions of pounds of profit. Imagine how much money you could give to God and the poor, the homeless, and those in need of medical supplies in the Third World, etc. Imagine how much you, your family, and your friends would have even after you had given much away to Jesus. You could live a wonderful life, debt free – no loans, no mortgage. You could pay cash for anything you wanted: clothes, houses, cars, food, holidays, etc., for your wife, children, relatives, friends, and Christian family. Or, just bless someone with a new house or car or holiday simply because you wanted to, just to make them happy!

I desire this, don't you? God desires this for you (who give to Jesus to spread the gospel). It is His will – not my idea but God's idea. It's written. So why should anyone want to argue with God about receiving prosperity? And for those among you who can't or won't or find it hard to think of exactly a hundred times what you gave being given back to you, then read Mark 10: 27–30. Jesus has promised at least many times more than what you give. Whatever you can accept from God, think big, and expect big blessings. In chapter 6, "Covenant Prosperity Promises", I pray that you will see why I wrote this chapter.

Don't be deceived by what people say about God not wanting people blessed with prosperity, that it is evil and bad for you. This is nothing but heresy, false teaching, and the twisting of Scripture. Church traditions say, "We are just poor sinners, saved by grace, by the favour of God, and surely God would not want us to have much, just our basic needs?" So take in this knowledge: in the Bible there are two important aspects to know without doubt. God said some things, and people said other things in the Scriptures. Once you personally know the promises of God, exactly what God promised you, then no one can deceive you into believing their deception or lies, their traditions, through lack of knowledge. Remember, the Bible is truth, and everything in it is truthfully stated or reported, but not everything is a statement or report of truth.

What God said and promised = truth. Once you know what God has commanded and promised, believe it, do it, and don't ever let it go! Don't ever let anyone persuade you to let go of your blessings, your rewards, and your harvest promised to you by God in the Bible. In 2 Timothy 2: 14–16, God, through Paul said to avoid godless chatter. Avoid vain babbling, pointless arguments, quarrels about religion, and issues which are disputable and unimportant. That's because these arguments can, if you let them or if you get involved with them, steal your peace or steal the truth of God's Word from you and leave you with fear and deception. The Greek word used here in verse 16 was *spermalogos*, which more accurately means, don't let people pick out of you your seed/truth and replace it with and leave you with their worthless droppings (false information). Don't let them take your seed and leave you with the equivalent of bird droppings.

If anyone in your life disputes with you over healing or prosperity, tell them that you have not got time to argue – but say it respectfully, go your way, and pray for them. Ask that the Lord will reveal to them the truth of His promises concerning prosperity and healing for them and will give them wisdom and understanding. Pray for them; don't argue! Spread your truth with those to whom the Lord leads you, with those who want to listen and want to be blessed. Amen! I repeat, don't throw your pearls (knowledge of the covenant promises) before swine (people who argue with you) about God's will for health, long life, and mental, financial, and material prosperity. Jesus said they will only trample them (the words you speak, which are the pearls) into the ground.

Think: earthly pearls are expensive. Which one of you would throw white pearls, worth a fortune, into a pigpen at the local farm? None of you! In the same way, God's treasure, His Word, should only be shared with those who you sense in your heart will quietly listen.

I'm not saying don't tell people about Jesus and his promises; just don't argue with people who don't want to listen. However, if someone says they don't understand or they've heard things like this before from other believers or other religions and are genuinely confused as to whether God wants everyone healed and prosperous, then explain your truth to them quietly and peacefully with joy. I pray the Lord will open your spirit, your heart, your eyes to see, to know to whom you really should teach God's word in love. Just pray yourself; ask Jesus to lead you to the right people at the right time (God's time), in the right place, and to give you the right words to speak to them. He will.

Just know you are God's sons and daughters in Christ if you have asked Jesus into your life. You are heirs to the promises, as stated in Galatians 3: 29. You are loved by God and have a right to inherit everything God has promised. Romans 8: 14–17 says if Jesus' Spirit is in you, you are God's child. You are heir to God's promises and inherit them all for free. God loves you and has wonderful things for you. Check out Galatians 3:12-29 (key verses are verses 13 and 14) and 4:4-7. Jesus loves us so much. He died for you so you could live, be His sons and daughters, have faith in Him, and trust what He says about what He promised to you, an heir (a beneficiary) loved by God. Hallelujah! He loved you enough even to suffer and die for you so that you could receive your inheritance, everything God promised to Abraham and his Seed, Jesus! Only you don't have to die; you can live and enjoy all God's promised blessings.

That's why Jesus appeared to the apostle Paul on the road to Damascus (see Acts 26: 15–18): to tell Paul that "I am sending you to be my servant for this purpose, to tell people that you have seen Me and to deliver what I (Jesus) will show you, reveal to you, teach you. I'm sending you to them to open their eyes, to turn them from darkness to light, from not knowing God's ways, promises, and light to delivering them from Satan's power and the curses of death, sickness, hell, and poverty. It's so they will receive forgiveness of their sins and receive a place in God's kingdom along with those who are sanctified, separated from Satan's darkness and his power by faith in Me, Jesus, and what I did for them, dying in their place so that they will receive eternal life and their inheritance."

The whole book of Galatians, six small chapters, explains a lot about this. It will take you about half an hour to read, and it explains exactly what Jesus told Paul to tell us. Take the time to read these chapters. Your eyes will be opened to what is yours by covenant right. Half an hour is not a long time. Jesus lives in you by His Spirit, and you can hear His voice. He will teach you all things. You don't need any ignorant people to teach you what God hasn't said, because you can hear His voice inside you saying, "That's from Me." Jesus says in John 10: 27, "My sheep hear my voice" (in their hearts and in their minds). You just know if something is from Jesus or not! You just know in your heart that's the voice of God in you.

First Corinthians 2: 16 tells us that we who are in Christ have the mind of Christ (the same mind as Christ the Anointed One): an anointed mind, the same as Jesus has.

Question: What was Jesus anointed (covered) with?

Answer: The Holy Spirit and power. Acts 10: 38 says so, and if you have asked Jesus to baptize you (cover or anoint you) with His Spirit, you have the same power and anointing that Jesus had on Him. Jesus had the Holy Spirit without measure; nevertheless, you have been given a measure of His power – enough for you to do all that God has called you to do for Him and enough to reveal to you all that God has promised you in his covenant agreement. All you need to do after asking Jesus into your life is obey the leading of the Holy Spirit and spend time studying the Word (the Bible's commands and promises). Ask God to explain them fully to you, in a way you can understand. The choice is yours: prosperity or lack, health or sickness, heaven or hell; you choose. I have chosen Jesus and His ways. I can't make you do the same, and neither will God force you, but He does ask, even beg you to come. Avoid hell, come to Jesus! Jesus loves you and longs to bless you. Come to Jesus. Receive Him and His blood sacrifice for you. Amen.

CHAPTER 6

COVENANT PROSPERITY PROMISES

At last, let's get down to what God Himself promised with regard to prosperity and the true meaning of prosperity. Prosperity is not just about money. No! Money comes from having a mind prospered by God, by His thoughts on life and wealth, which you can find in His Word, the Bible. I'm not saying God does not want you prospered with money and lots of it, as doubtless He does. But being prosperous in finances is not just going to come instantly, like a lightning bolt. There are some things you have to do first in order to receive money, lots of money, and nice possessions, like cars, houses, holidays, clothes, the best food, and much more: goods to use which bring pleasure to you personally. This prosperity would also include health and being well, because if you have cancer or are in constant pain and crippled, mentally ill or depressed, what good are money and nice things. You need both.

God's Word reveals to us how to acquire them. Thank God there are many promises on this subject. The Bible is full of them. Blessing His people is one of God's favourite subjects. We start in the New Covenant with 3 John 2 which says, "Beloved, I wish (desire) above all things that you may prosper and be in health, even as your soul prospers." The true meaning of the Greek word translated *soul* is more accurately translated into English as "mind, will, and emotion".

Your mind has the ability to learn, retain, and use information. Your will is in your mind or soul. Therefore, once you learn or know something, you can choose by an act of your free will either to act on what you learned or not to act. Your soul is housed in your spirit, and your spirit is housed in your body. You are a spirit being with a mind living inside a flesh, bone, and blood body. Your flesh or body only does what your mind tells it to do, good or bad. They are three but housed in one body.

Suppose your mind thinks that you should tidy the garden. You have to choose whether or not to actually tidy the garden. You may not feel like doing it but know you should, as the garden is overgrown. That's where your will comes in, will power. You decide to tidy the garden, so your body moves into action. You can overrule your emotions, even if you may not feel like doing the work. Emotions may tell you to watch TV and tidy the garden tomorrow. The next day comes, and you still feel like putting off the work. That's what the Bible says is your flesh taking over – yes, your flesh body ruling your mind. The diligent people will watch TV after they have tidied the garden. This takes a choice and an act of your will to overrule your flesh and emotions.

What the Holy Spirit is saying in 3 John 2 is that the more of God's words, ways, knowledge, promises, and commands that your mind learns and decides to put into practice, the more God says your mind is prospering. The New Testament Greek word translated into English as *prosper* actually means "to increase in, to have much more of". Thus, your mind prospering means your mind is increasing in knowledge and wisdom of God's Word. Your prosperity means you increase in goods, property, and money. Your body increases in good health, and God's healing fire flows in you. Amen!

So whether you feel like it or not, I strongly recommend that you make time each day to study the Bible. Start with at least half an hour per day, and invest time praying and asking God to explain to you the truth of what you are reading. Make it an act of your will, and start to experience the prosperity.

Can you see the link between 3 John 2 and Matthew 6:33, which says, "seek instead the kingdom of God, and all these things will be added to you" by God without you spending all your mind, time, and effort chasing them? Also Luke 11:29,30 says, "And do not set your heart on what you will eat or drink, do not worry about it. For the pagan world runs after all such things, and your heavenly Father knows that you need them.but seek His kingdom and these things will be given to you as well." Thank and praise the Lord right after you ask Him for the understanding and wisdom. This shows Him and it also shows you that you believed you received the wisdom and understanding when you asked Him for it. Mark 11: 23–24 says, "Believe you receive (whatsoever) you ask for when (as soon as) you pray." Ask God for anything, and you shall have whatever you say – whatever God promises in His covenant with over 7,000 promises, including promises of long life, protection, finances, lands, and health. These are only a few of the things you can pray for and believe and say that you have them.

Keep this spiritual truth going. Whenever you ask for anything, believe you receive it, and expect God to give it now, right now. Sometimes things come quickly and sometimes more slowly, but they do always come to those who have faith in God to bring His Word to pass. Just be patient, and things will change for the better. Do in faith as He directs, and the bad things will change for good, okay?

That's all there is to it. Don't make it more complicated. Don't worry if you slip up and say something doubtful or negative. Just tell God, "Hey, Lord, I'm sorry; forgive me. I just got a bit down. I receive Your love and forgiveness." It only takes ten seconds: simply confess to the Lord that you missed it, and then you can then start again. Do your utmost to stay focused on the promise and not on the problem.

Keep the Word before your eyes and going into your ears. As Romans 10: 17 says, because "Faith comes by hearing and hearing by God's word." That's why you need to hear yourself say you have it, because faith rises up in you and fills your heart and mind, and doubt is pushed out.

Don't let yourself hear too much of other people's negative talk; it rubs off on you. Spend time alone with God or with other believers like yourself. Go where believers in Jesus and His promises go, then your faith will grow.

You must have faith to receive from God, and faith only comes by hearing – hearing daily; even if it's only half an hour to start with, it grows on you. The more you hear, the more you want to hear, because what you hear is good news for you, and what you hear brings you hope. The Greek New Testament word we translate as *hope* means "being certain of receiving and having, an earnest expectation of that thing". Now you get up every day looking for it. Your base or foundation for expecting or hoping is now focused on God's faithfulness and love to do what He said. You know inside that the Lord has the power, the riches and the resources to do what He said and promised. Amen.

In 1 Corinthians 13: 13 the apostle Paul said that faith, hope, and love are the most important things that we as believers in Jesus can ever have. It says in 1 John 4: 16 that "God is love, and God and His love are in you." This is important in receiving from God.

Read this next Scripture in your own Bible, think on it, and let it sink into your heart and your mind. Mull over it, and meditate on it. Hebrews 11: 1–3, in key verse 1, says, "Faith is the substance (stuff) of things hoped for, the evidence of things not (yet) seen." If you truly believe you have received, what comes next? In Mark 11: 25, the final command in receiving is this, said Jesus: "When you stand praying, if you hold anything against anyone, forgive him, so that your Father in heaven can forgive you your sins" (NIV). Your faith and hope work by love, as Galatians 5: 6 says. Love is the switch that turns on the light, so if you have unforgiveness in your heart, this is not love. Unforgiveness keeps your faith from receiving prosperity from God. When you have forgiven, you can call in your prosperity. Praise God, there are over 7,000 promises on prosperity, health, long life, and protection from enemies by Him and His angels. They are promises about the power to do miracles through you; eternal life; and riches in money, goods, property, lands, gold and silver, the riches and hidden riches (not yet found) *on and in this earth to have now.* We can be *fully convinced* that God wants us wealthy with nothing missing.

When Jews, even today, encounter a friend or neighbour, they say, "Shalom." It means "I wish you to be complete, full, with nothing missing, having peace of mind". When a Jew greets a fellow Jew with "Shalom", and the other person says, "No", it means something is missing. Because Jews are covenant minded, they then help one another secure whatever they need. They know God has commanded it ("Love your neighbour as yourself") and that God will bless His people (Jews or people in Christ) when they bless others. To bless means "to increase someone in goods, money, help, love, etc.". Jesus Himself said to His disciples on earth in John 14: 27, "My peace (he spoke in Hebrew and Aramaic), My shalom I leave with you. I'm going to heaven, and I'm leaving you with blessings of shalom, nothing missing. You are My covenant brothers, washed in

My blood, made the righteousness of God. You have right standing with God the Father." (Check out Romans 3: 21–25, especially key verse 25, and Galatians 3: 29.)

Revelation 21: 1–5 tells us that we receive the inheritance spoken of in Galatians 3: 28–29 right now, here on earth. That's why Jesus Himself said in Mark 10: 29–30, "There is no one who has left house or brothers or sisters or father or mother or wife or children or lands for My sake and the gospel's, who will not fail to receive back as a harvest a hundredfold, now in this age, on earth." When God directs you to give, please obey and give. That's His command. Give where the Holy Spirit (the Spirit of Jesus) directs, and give the amount He tells you, and God promises that you will receive a hundredfold increase.

You don't believe me? Then let's look at Mark 10: 29–30, Matthew 19: 16–22, and Galatians 3:29. The key verse in Matthew 19 is verse 21. We are talking here about sowing and reaping. The rich young ruler came to Jesus to ask what he must do to inherit eternal life. "Sell what you have and give to the poor" was Jesus' response (the young man's riches had him, not the other way round), so that he would have treasure in heaven – for where your treasure is there will your heart be also (see Matt. 6: 21). Peter in Matthew 19: 27 said, "We have left everything and followed you." It's after that statement that Jesus promises hundredfold return.

In 2 Corinthians 9 Paul was dealing with the Corinthian assembly's giving their finances to other Christians in Jerusalem who were in great difficulties. In verses 6–8 he encouraged them to sow bountifully – not grudgingly, but to be hilarious givers – and God would make all grace (all favour) abound towards them so that they would have all sufficiency in all things and have an abundance for every good work. Verses 9–11 include a quotation from Psalm 112: 9 ("He has dispersed abroad, he has given to the poor, His righteousness endures for ever"). These verses apply to those who give generously, promising that they shall reap bountifully. In Philippians 4: 14–19 Paul's letter told the church that they had done well in sharing in his distress, that they were the only ones who shared in giving and receiving, and that it would be credited to their account. As a result, verse 19 promised, all their needs would be supplied. Notice they understood receiving their harvest after giving generous seed.

In Galatians 6: 6–10 Paul's letter teaches about receiving instruction in the Word, that we must share all good things with our instructor. People reap what they sow. We are encouraged not to grow weary in doing good, because we will reap if we do not give up – the harvest is coming!

First though, the Word of God tells us to give a tithe or tenth of the first fruits of all our income to God. This is the first step in receiving the full inheritance from God. You must realise that tithing is not giving; the one tenth or tithe already belongs to God. We just return to God the tithe. Malachi 3: 10 tells us that the Lord opens the floodgates of heaven's blessings on the tither! That's good news. However, don't confuse tithing with giving offerings. The definition of giving for the gospel's sake is the offering of an amount of your choice from the 90 per cent that's left after you tithe. It's a gift that *you offer freely* or give as God directs you to the ministry or individuals of His choosing.

Think about this. Abraham tithed before the Law was given! He tithed of the spoil he had won in a battle to Melchizedek, King of Salem (wholeness, nothing wanting, nothing missing). Abraham wouldn't take anything except what his men had eaten. Tithing is the acknowledgement that God is our provider. Although we are not under the curse of the Law, as promised in Galatians 3: 13, if you do not give anything or give very little, you will experience a lack of money and material goods, even though you are redeemed personally from financial lack. You will not be living in the good of the blessing. In Luke 6: 38 Jesus said, "Give, and it will be given back to you with the same measure that you use." You choose the measure, big or small.

Now I will share with you the Scriptures, promises, and commands on seed time, harvest time, tithing, and giving because it's part of the covenant or agreement, which is a two-way matter. You do as God says, and after that, God will give you the promised thirty-, sixty-, or hundredfold return, *now, on earth*. So we can see here this is not an easy way. It's not just about having pennies from heaven and financial riches dropping out of the sky on you. Please, *please* get this. It is a serious thing that most, though not all, Christians miss. When we do not tithe, return to God what is rightfully His, we rob God, steal from Him. Although we will still go to heaven after receiving Jesus into our lives, we will live under a financial curse *on earth now.* This is true especially for those people who fully understand that they should tithe but won't or don't.

Read Malachi 3: 6–17 to get the whole picture. Now we will look at the key verses 7–11:

> "Ever since the times of your forefathers you have turned away from My decrees and have not kept them. Return to Me and I will return to you," says the Lord Almighty.
>
> "But you ask, 'How are we to return?'
>
> "Will a man rob God? Yet you rob Me in tithes and offerings."

(Deuteronomy 28: 15–68 demonstrates that the whole nation of Israel is under a curse because those who don't tithe are robbing God.)

> "Bring the whole tithe into the storehouse so that there will be food in the My house. Test me in this," says the Lord Almighty, "and see if I will not throw open upon (for you, the tithers) the floodgates of heaven and pour out so much blessing that you shall not have room enough (in your storehouse) for it. I will prevent pests from devouring your crops (I will rebuke the devourer, the devil, for your sake), and the vines (bearing grapes) in your fields will not cast their fruit."

(All your previous planting and hard work *will* bear fruit and produce harvests, instead of the grapes falling off the vines before they are ripe, big and ready.)

Did Jesus say in the New Testament that we should tithe? Let's look at Luke 11: 39–42. The key verse is verse 42. Read in your own Bible. I read here that Jesus Himself said that *we should tithe* to God, give the tenth. Jesus said, "Now you Pharisees make the outside of the cup and dish clean but your inward part is full of greed and wickedness …. But rather give alms of what you have." "Give what is inside the dish (give what you have) to the poor, and then everything will be clean and right for you."

Jesus said to the Jewish leaders (verse 42, NIV), "Woe to you Pharisees, because you give God a tenth of your (crops), mint, rue and all other kinds of garden herbs, but you neglect justice and the love of God. You should have practiced the latter (love, mercy, justice for all people) *without leaving the former* (tenth to God) *undone."*

The Pharisees tithed but didn't have love for God's people; they were hard-hearted, mistreating the ordinary people on the streets. Jesus said trouble would come to them even though they tithed. See how *faith works by love?* I pray that you will see. The Jewish leaders were obeying God in tithing but treating people terribly, and Jesus told them this would stop the floodgates of heaven's blessings coming to them. Instead, trouble would come. Jesus said you must tithe and display love, justice, mercy, and a forgiving heart. Tithing alone will not result in the abundance or flood of God's blessings into your life. You must have love for God and His people, being prepared to give to and help the poor and needy. *You must offer help.* Tithe and give help, and then the promise of abundance will be poured out on you by God.

So then, think of it this way. When you confess your faults, sins, and wrongs to God, He immediately forgives you. God forgives them all. So you also can forgive everyone who has hurt or offended you. You can say, "Okay, Jesus, I forgive that person. Please heal my hurts." Then decide to walk in love. Simply ask God to lead you to the people, ministries, or charities He wants you to support. Now you can return to God His tenth and give offerings over and above this, as much as you decide. Fully expect the Lord to keep His promise to open the windows of heaven and pour out on you and your house His blessings and increase because you tithed and gave love offerings to His people and His work. Just ask God to show you, through His Holy Spirit, where to give and how much, and He will do the rest. You will know that you know that you know, deep within your spirit.

When you first start tithing and giving offerings in faith according to the promise in Malachi 3: 10 and have checked you're forgiving and walking in love the best you can, then you will notice immediately the following:

Your remaining money after tithes and offerings seems to go much further. You find bargains coming your way; you appear to be able to buy more than before. This is just the beginning of your blessings and harvests. Things that seemed to go wrong previously now go right as you continue to tithe and give offerings. It's important to tithe and give offerings every week, or every month or even daily as you get paid, never using this money to pay your bills or for family pleasures in any way. This money is for God's work, to spread the gospel, and to help the poor and the lost. When you do this in faith, fully expecting God's abundant blessings each day, you will see the enormous riches of God manifested to you, in your bank account, in your hand and home, despite how good or bad things *appear* to be.

But you cannot – I repeat, you cannot *try tithing and offering for a trial period to see if it works, to verify whether God will bless you. Why? Because this shows lack of faith and trust in what God said in Hebrews 11: 1 and what Jesus said and promised in Mark 10: 29–30:* not that God might bless you, but that He *will* bless you mightily as long as you decide to tithe and give for life, every week, not as a trial, stopping if money is a bit tight. Tithing is a commitment. Your giving is a statement of faith, without which if your blessing doesn't appear instantly, you will give up. You can't just "try it".

The principle of giving has not passed away. God tells us in Malachi 3: 10 to test Him in this. Satan tries to attack your finances in the hope that you will stop, thus preventing your blessings and harvests. Don't let Satan fool you if things seem to be a bit tight financially. God is not testing you; James 1:13, 16-17 says, "Let no man say when he is tempted (tested and tried) that it is God for God tests no-one. This is an attack of Satan. Loose my money. I cast out the demons behind poverty, lack, and debt. I bind you. You cannot steal my God-given blessings and finances, now or ever again, in Jesus' name. I trust God, and the Lord will do for me all that He promised, and I believe Him, not you. So, according to Hebrews 11: 1, *faith is the substance of things hoped for,* or being certain of what we do not yet see."

Remember, the Hebrew word for hope is "earnest trusting in God's Word". It's *expectation, knowing without doubt that God will do exactly what you hope for.* The reward is based on your trust in God, not on your giving the money. People give money and other things every day, but they never get a thirty-, sixty-, or hundredfold reward. Only those who give because God commanded it and believe with expectation that God will reward them (because He said that He would) are the ones who will receive every time. Hebrews 11: 6 says, "Without faith in Him it is impossible to please

God. You must believe that God exists and that He rewards those who earnestly seek him." Go to Him in faith, expecting Him to reward you for being a hearer and doer of His Word. Why? Because it is impossible for you to please God if you will not use your faith in Him and what He said. You must choose by an act of your will to say, "I will believe and do what God says (tithe and give), and I will receive what God promised me. I will trust Him; I will have faith in Him." *You* have to decide with *your* free will to do this.

Remember, just saying a promise of God every day for a year will not alone bring the blessing. *You must also have believe in your heart* that the promise that you both read and heard will be given to you. This is the way faith is released: *belief in the heart and confession with the mouth.*

Let's go back for a moment to the early chapters of this book. Remember how God had a law of the spirit of life in Christ Jesus which has set me free fom the law of sin and death? Believe in your heart and confess with your mouth, then it comes to pass. Take a few minutes to consider the following question. How did you get delivered from the kingdom of darkness and translated into the kingdom of His dear Son? You believed in your heart that Jesus the Christ died for you and that God the Father raised Him from the dead, and with your mouth, you confessed Jesus as your Lord and Saviour. Then, instantly, you were saved, born again; the Holy Spirit came into you, bringing you into the experience of the new birth, whereby you became a new creation in Christ Jesus. Catch this: *the law of the Spirit* worked.

The same law works with *all God's promises*. Keep the command by giving for the sake of Jesus, and inherit the promise by receiving your harvest here and now on earth, in your lifetime. Jesus said in Matthew 12: 34 that "out of the abundance of the heart, the mouth speaks." In other words, what your heart is full of, this is what you will speak about. Jesus said the hearts of the religious teachers were full of evil, and so they spoke evil things. They wanted Jesus dead, because He was teaching the people how to receive God's promises by following His instruction, but the Pharisees were jealous of Jesus and afraid for their future position and safety. Jesus wasn't giving them a new way of life but an understanding of how to get ready for the advent of the New Covenant prophesied in the Old Testament in Ezekiel 36 and Jeremiah 31: 31–34. Jesus made Himself a servant (see Phil. 2: 5–11) and laid aside His majesty and privileges. He was the first Man to live fully under the Abrahamic covenant, under the anointing of the Holy Spirit.

Why do I use this illustration of the jealous and evil religious leaders? It's because you can choose what teachings enter your ears, heart, and mind. Good or evil, faith or fear, God's Word and His promises or human religious traditions – whatever enters your heart in abundance will come out from your mouth in abundance, and then you will receive a harvest in abundance because of the Law of the Spirit. Please put the prosperity promises into your heart by daily reading them in the Bible as well as faith-filled magazines and books, by ministers such as Kenneth Copeland, Jerry Savelle, John Avenzini, Joseph Prince, and Andrew Wommack or by listening to tapes or CDs.

Most importantly, listen to yourself speaking aloud the prosperity promises, which will sink into your heart and spirit and come out from your mouth mixed with faith in the power and ability of God to perform His Word in your life. Faith comes by hearing and hearing by God's Word. You can only put an abundant overflow of faith into your heart by hearing God's Word and in this case by hearing God's promises on prosperity.

Hold on to this unchangeable truth: God cannot and will not lie. You can trust Him. John 1: 1 and 1: 14 tell us that Jesus is God, the living Word, come to earth in the flesh. Hebrews 13: 8–9 declares that Jesus, who is God's Word in the flesh, is the same yesterday, today, (John1:1,2.) and forever. We read in Matthew 24: 35 that Jesus, who is God the Word, said, "Heaven and earth will pass away, but my words will never pass away." His promise will work for you today, tomorrow, and forevermore, in all situations and circumstances. Hallelujah. It's time to shout out, *Glory to God.*

All the prosperity promises are true, and you will receive them now, here on earth *as long as you follow exactly God's instructions on giving.* You will be able to give to every good work and be a blessing to others and still have plenty for yourself and loved ones. Take your time and read Deuteronomy 28:1-14 now before you read the rest of this page. Do you see the wonderful promises given to you and your family?

Fix God's promises and commandments in your heart and mind; keep them before your eyes. Write them down, place them where you can see and read them often, and teach these promises to your loved ones. Read them in your Bible as you're able, and know that your days will be many, with long life in the land flowing with milk and honey as promised by God – overflowing with prosperity just as God swore on oath to Abraham and his Seed, Jesus and his descendants. That's you in Christ. Remember, it is vital that you take to heart and follow the instructions given by God.

"How can we start to do this?", I hear you ask. Psalm 128:1-2 in the Amplified version says, "Blessed (happy, fortunate, to be envied) is everyone who fears, reveres and worships the Lord, who walks in His ways and lives according to His commandments. For you shall eat (the fruit) of the labour of your hands; happy (blessed, fortunate, enviable) shall you be, and it shall be well with you" What exactly is the fear of the Lord? Look at Proverbs 8: 13, which says, "The fear of the Lord is to hate evil: pride, and arrogancy, and the evil way, and the froward (deceitful) mouth do I hate." So to prosper you must fear God. This does not mean being terrified of Him. To fear God in the Hebrew here means "to keep yourself from doing evil". Stop doing the things which are wrong and bad. No more violence, people baiting, or badmouthing your husband or wife, especially in front of others. No more stealing, false testimony, adultery.

How can we live up to such high standards and keep all His instructions? The answer is twofold. Firstly, with the help of the Holy Spirit you can. Jesus died and rose again so that He could live inside you. Secondly, make a choice to do things God's way. This is not easy, but with the Holy Spirit's help, it's much easier than you think. Believe me, I have experienced the Holy Spirit's help. *Praise God.* As Jesus said in Matthew 11: 28–30 (NIV), "Come to me, *all* you who are weary and (who are) burdened (and heavy laden), and I (Jesus) will give you rest. Take My yoke (you invite Jesus into you) upon you and learn from Me, for I am gentle and humble in heart, and you will find rest for your soul. For My yoke is easy and My burden is light."

Question: What are the yoke and the burden?

Answer: A *yoke* is a coupling of chain, metal, or wood, which links something or someone together in bondage or slavery – two oxen made to pull a load, for instance. The *burden* is a heavy weight or load which is difficult or nearly impossible to carry. You might be yoked to alcoholism or another addiction, poverty, debt, or an unhappy marriage or job, and because you are tied to it you cannot break free. Eventually this wears you down; it is a burden that you can no longer carry.

Well, in Matthew 11: 28–30 Jesus said, "Hey, come on, people, come to me, *all* who are yoked and laden with heavy burdens, and I will give you in exchange My yoke. You will be tied to Me, and My burden is light. You can learn from Me, and you will have the blessings of Almighty God tied to you." *Glory.* What has this to do with prosperity and the fear of the Lord? Simply this: it is absolutely impossible to be perfect and keep *all* God's commands *all* the time, *Impossible!* Jesus Christ is the only perfect one, the Lamb without spot or blemish. Jesus became a curse for our sins, taking everything upon Himself so that the blessing promised to Abraham and his Seed would come on the Gentiles. He broke the curse and delivered us from death through His death and resurrection, and He is a blessing so that we can now be blessed, through Jesus Christ in us, having invited Him into our hearts and lives and confessed with our mouths that He is our Lord and Saviour. Hence, the heavy burden too heavy for us to bear is now carried by Jesus. This means that we are no longer under the curse of the Law and no longer under the judgment and condemnation of God.

Of course we are still flesh and blood, so what should we do when we sin? Read 1 John 1: 5–10 and 2: 1–2, where the Word explains that if we confess our sins from the heart and ask for forgiveness in the name of Jesus, our God, who is just, merciful, and righteous, will forgive us. Jesus Himself will speak to God the Father on our behalf and in our defence, saying that He has paid the price for us. We know and love Jesus when we keep His commands. So when you sin in moments of weakness, simply go to Jesus, tell Him how sorry you are, and ask the Holy Spirit to help you and change you with His refining fire. God will forgive you and then remember your sins no more because of who you are in Jesus Christ. Proverbs 10: 22 (NIV) offers this great promise: "The blessing of the Lord brings *wealth* (material and financial), and He (God) adds no trouble (or sorrow) to it."

Question: Does religious tradition say that lots of money brings trouble and sorrow?

Answer: Yes.

Question: Does God's Word say money from God brings trouble or sorrow?

Answer: No, none, no trouble at all. See the difference between what God and His Word say about money and wealth and what religious people say, who either don't know what God has said, or do know yet continue for some reason to promote the opposite of what He says.

Question: How do we get (or receive) all this wealth from God yet have it without any sorrow or trouble coming with it?

Answer: By obeying God on tithing and giving. Proverbs 3: 9–10 (NIV) says, "Honour the Lord (God/Jesus) with your wealth (your money), (and) with the *first fruits* (the first 10 per cent) of all your crops (income and goods); then your barns (storehouses and bank accounts, etc.) will be filled to overflowing, and your vats will brim over (overflow) with new wine." Do you see it? First and best goes to God. You no longer love money but love God, and you prove it to Him and yourself by honouring Him with your best giving and the first fruits of your income and material goods!

The Hebrews (in ancient times, even in Jesus' time on earth) saw wine, according to God's Word, as a source of pleasure, joy, and a divine gift, bringing joy and a happy, merry heart. The Bible, God's Word, condemns drunkenness, so don't get drunk! If you're addicted to drink, don't panic! Ask Jesus to help you, to deliver you; trust Him, and He will. Deuteronomy 7: 13, Psalm 104: 15, Hosea 2: 8, Jeremiah 31: 12, Joel 3: 18, and Amos 9: 13–14 explain the relationship of joy to new wine. This promise is your new wine; newly given riches bringing joy and a merry heart. Happiness, not sorrow, will overflow in your life. Praise God when you have no more debt and can pay your bills without worry, when you can buy a house, clothes, and a car, paying cash for them all without borrowing. Because you don't love the money more than you love God, the money now becomes a tool to be used for the good of others.

This is very important, and I need to stress it. You can do what Jesus commanded in Mark 10: 29–30. All who give for His sake and the spreading of the gospel now, on earth in this age, will receive a hundredfold (or thirty- or sixtyfold) or whichever they can believe Him for. God's best is to give us the hundredfold to bless others!

Malachi 3: 10–12 declares that you can choose to test God after you tithe and see for yourself if God will not throw open the floodgates of heaven and pour out so much blessing (more than is needed) that you will not have enough room for it in your place of storage (house, bank accounts, etc.). Verses 11–12 say that even the people of other nations will see it and say you are blessed!

Question: If the world's economy collapsed, how could God get all of the best things, like food, homes, lands, etc., even luxuries to me?

Answer: Psalm 24: 1 says this. "The earth and all that's in it belongs to me, says the Lord." Haggai 2:8 (NIV) states, "'The silver is mine and the gold is mine,' declares the Lord Almighty." They don't belong to governments. Consequently, God has a right to give them to His children who choose to test Him and see if He will not pour out the flood of blessings on them.

Trust and test God in this matter, and see for yourself. You will always be able to give help to others to whom the Holy Spirit directs you, whether it be to family and friends; to the church, for spreading the gospel; or to the homeless, the sick, or the poverty stricken. You should bless all the families of the earth. Genesis 12: 1–3, 7 says it is God's will for Abraham and his seed forever. God is a good and generous God, and He uses His people as His hands to give out His goods to whom He wants, when He wants. You always reap a harvest on what you sow. Give much, reap much. Give only a little, and your reaping will be meagre. Second Corinthians 9: 6–7 confirms this. Jesus said it, so argue with Him, not with me, but it's best you agree with Him. I am only passing on to you what He said, so agree with me instead of arguing.

Do your giving with a cheerful heart. If you can't get happy about how much you give, then give less. To give grudgingly or under fear will cause you stress. In those circumstances it's better giving less and being cheerful.

The Lord loves a cheerful giver. When you give happily and are joyful about giving to God, you please Him, "and God is able to make every (all) grace (favour) abound to you so that always, in all things, at all times, everywhere, always, at home or abroad you will have an abundance for every good work" (see 2 Cor. 9: 8). Having all that you need, you will be able to give, abound in all God's work of giving. People will praise and thank God for your generous sharing with them and with everyone else whom God leads you to. These people who have received God's gifts through you will pray for your needs and desires to be met by Him (through others) because of the grace (abundant favour) God has given you.

Thanks be to God for His indescribable gift (see 2 Cor. 9: 15) of your new loving nature and born-again spirit in Jesus Christ, which causes you to be so generous, unlike most people in this world, who love and desire money and keep it for themselves. So even the desire to give to God, His people, the poor, the needy, homeless, suffering, refugees, etc., is a gift from God. Indescribable! Why? Because the desire in Christ to give goes against normal human nature, which is in our bones, our genes, our flesh, descending from our fallen fleshly (earthly desiring) father, Adam. In Christ you get a new heart, you're born again, and you desire the things of God now. That's because your new Father is God, who created in your body a new spirit being that did not exist in you before you asked Jesus into your heart.

Second Corinthians 5: 17 says we are a new creation! It's not just a new start; that is not what this Scripture means. Pray it out. Pray and ask the Lord to explain and reveal to you the truth of His Word that you are reading. Study it in your own Bible until you get a revelation of it in your heart, not just your head. God loves all people, but He must be sad, grieved, by those who will not believe Him for anything. This is like saying, "Lord, I know You said it in Your Word. It is written there, but I don't really believe in my heart that You will do it for me." God will forgive your unbelief if you just confess it to Him, say you are sorry, and ask Him to help you to believe. If you don't believe God and His Word, you're sinning, because whatever is not of faith is sin (Romans 14: 23). Don't get mad at me; I didn't write this. God did, through his servant, Paul. Not believing in what God says and promises is wrong. It's what God calls sin. It's just as much sin as all the other sins.

Do you see it? I pray that you do see it in your spirit and understand it in your mind (you have the mind of Christ), your sound mind. What makes your mind full of soundness, firm in His foundation? Second Timothy 1:7 gives us the answer; sound teaching of God's Word and promise. 1 Corinthians 2:16 tells us that we have the mind of Christ. This is how our soul (mind, will, emotions) prospers. Third John 2 says you will prosper and be in good health even as your soul-mind prospers. Can you see the link between receiving and increasing prosperity in finances, health, in all areas of life and increasing your sound mind with God's Word?

I have experienced many harvest times after my wife and I gave over our tithe to either a ministry or a needy person (to whom Jesus instructed us to give). Sometimes the return, or harvest, has come quickly, a week or month after we gave, sometimes six months or a year later, but it always comes at just the right time for us, when we either need or desire it most. Trust my testimony.

But above all trust God's Word. Ask Jesus to be your Lord, Master and Saviour! Ask Jesus to fill you and baptise you in His Holy Spirit and power. Without Jesus you are not saved, and you will go to hell. Ask Jesus into your life, okay? Without the baptism of the Holy Spirit you will struggle because the baptism of the Holy Spirit empowers us to serve God and receive from Him. The power only comes from the Holy Spirit in you. All you have to do is ask and say, "Jesus, come into my heart and baptise me with your Holy Spirit power with signs following." If you have not yet done it, then do so and get baptised in water in Jesus' name. Don't just be sprinkled but, as the Word of God commands, under water, just as Jesus did. Find a Bible-believing church to do this for you. Simply ask Jesus which church to go to, which church is best for you, and expect Him to put you there.

It's all a happy and joyful experience. You still have your own mind. God's Spirit will not forcibly possess you. He will help you, prompt you, and tell you what to do and where to go. Yet the choice of whether to do it or not will still be yours. It's up to you to choose to obey the Lord. As for me, I will choose to do it and be blessed and prospered. So do it! Just do it! Amen!

CHAPTER 7

THE COVENANT AND PROTECTION

We now know that God wants us to be saved, then prosperous in all good things, going to heaven, never seeing death, having eternal life, knowing Jesus as Lord, and being changed by His Holy Spirit to act and think like Him. He wants us walking in love, peace, and joy and enjoying all He promised us in His covenant, sealed in the blood of Jesus, guaranteed as part of our inheritance. This is God's perfect will for us, His people, and anyone who will make Jesus their Lord and Saviour.

You know that God wants you well, never sick, or else healed if you are sick! You know God wants you to be prosperous, rich, to tithe, give, and receive thirty-, sixty-, or hundredfold harvests so you can be blessed and be a blessing to others. You know God wants you to be a good servant of Jesus, telling others the good news about Him and His word and teachings. You know God wants you to have a long life till you're satisfied, living seventy or eighty or even up to 120 years. Psalm 91: 16 says so.

Question: Why, if you know all these promises, would you not want to live your desired number of years, never sick, never in lack, and always serving Jesus?

Answer: Satan and his demons will use people and circumstances to maim, injure, or kill you. That's bad news.

Question: What's the good news?

Answer: God has a plan of protection but you must know it and then claim it by faith in the protection promises. You must say what you believe God will do for you. That's how you got born again. In Christ, you are an heir to the promises. You need to know these promises of God, believe them, and put them into your heart. Then, when spoken out of your mouth out loud so that you can hear the written promises, remember this: faith comes by hearing and hearing by the Word of God. In considering protection and preservation, bear in mind that you have bodyguards. They are called angels. They have been sent as ministers and servants to you, and that is their number-one purpose. Surprised? Let's read God's Word which tells us about this.

> Are they [angels] not all ministering spirits sent forth to minister for them who shall be heirs of salvation? (Heb. 1: 14)

Now how many Christians know that every good angel has been sent to help the people in Christ, who are the heirs or inheritors of salvation? The exact Greek word here translated *salvation* means "the promised wholeness of God". The protection of ministering angels is your inherited right when you belong to Jesus. Link Galatians 3: 29 to Hebrews 1: 14.

Your own personal angel has been sent to minister or to help, including protecting you, because it's part of your inheritance, won for you by Jesus, who shed His blood of the New Covenant for you. However, sadly, most of the church say things like "You never know, you might have an accident. Who knows? It could happen to anyone. Mrs Jones was only thirty years old and died suddenly crossing the road; she was hit by a truck - and she attended church twice a week!"

Remember, in Mark 11: 22–23 (NIV), Jesus said, "Have faith in God. I tell you the truth, if anyone says to this mountain, 'Go, throw yourself into the sea,' and does not doubt in his heart but believes that what he says will happen, it will be done for him." You will have to say it, so say, "Yes, Lord, angels will protect and help me and my household because You said so, and I both believe it and say it. Jesus said I will have what I say, and I say angels will protect and minister to me." Now, shout for joy! That's good news. Now you can know for certain that God is good.

We are going to look now at what God's people all have in common that brings this wonderful, godly, supernatural protection to them and their families. Let's look at Psalm 91: 1–2 (NIV), which says, "He who dwells in the shelter of the Most High will rest in the shadow of the Almighty. I will say of the Lord, 'He is my refuge and my fortress, my God, in whom I trust'."

Note this important point. He *dwells* in the shelter of the Most High God. This is important, readers. To dwell in your house, you live there. You go to work, and you come home again every night and live there, eat and drink there, sleep there. You don't live in your house one day a week and spend six days away from your dwelling place; that's not dwelling. No, you live or dwell in your house, and you probably lock your doors and windows, put your burglar alarm on, and then rest with peace of mind. This is what verse 1 of Psalm 91 is saying. *If you want Gods protection you have to dwell in the shelter of the Most High God. Then you will find rest under the shadow of the Almighty God.*

Question: How do you dwell in the shadow of the Almighty, finding rest and peace of mind, knowing no harm will come to you and your household?

Answer: You spend time with God daily, just the way you spend time at your house or spend time attending to your job or work.

Question: How do I spend time with God daily, seven days a week?

Answer: Simple. Spend time in prayer, talking to God, asking for his guidance for the day, taking time to listen to God's voice and hear His answer. Pray for others, especially the unsaved and oppressed. Spend time praising God, thanking Him for everything He has done for you. Worship Him for giving His life and shedding His blood for you. Tell Him you love Him because He first loved you. Tell Jesus you trust Him. Spend time reading the Bible. Ask God the Holy Spirit to show you what He's saying, and ask Him to show you His promises and how to get them to work for you. Ask Him for knowledge and wisdom. As you read His Word, things you never understood before will become clearer to you. Take time to tell others about Jesus and how they, too, can know Him. Answer their questions with the help of the Holy Spirit and the knowledge you have from reading the Word of God and His commands and promises. Ask God to lead you to the right person at the right time and to give you the right words and good deeds for that person. You will then be a blessing for the glory of Jesus.

Question: How long each day should I spend worshiping, praising, praying, reading my Bible, and sharing Jesus?

Answer: Whatever is comfortable to you. Each person is different. Do the best you can daily, not just on Sunday's and that's the key. Be a giver, tithing and giving offerings, asking the Lord where and to whom He wishes His money to go and expect the 100 fold harvest to come back to you. In God's sight you are now daily living, dwelling under His wings. In the shadow of the Almighty is where you live. Then verse 2 of Psalm 91 makes an entrance: "I (that's you) will say of you, Lord, You are my refuge and my fortress, my God in whom I trust." A fortress protects the people who live and dwell inside, and it becomes their refuge from the attacking army.

Now, let's look at true Bible reports of some people who lived daily in the shadow of the Almighty, by daily spending time, obeying God's instructions, praying, worshiping, and in fellowship, candidly telling others about Yahweh, Jehovah, the God of the Jews. Let's also see what they said in the face of death and serious danger. They told others that God would deliver them and, guess what, God always delivered them. Glory to God! Here are the names of some of them. Daniel, who was thrown into a lion's den with starving lions; God rescued him; no harm came to him. Shadrach, Meshach, and Abednego (Daniel's friends), were put into a fiery furnace that could smelt iron or bronze to liquid. God delivered them unharmed; even their clothes and hair were not singed!

Then there was Joseph, brought before the Egyptian pharaoh and told he would be put to death if he failed to discern Pharaoh's dream. God delivered him, and no harm came to him either. Later Joseph was put in charge of all Egypt, second in command only to Pharaoh. Moses and approximately two million Israelites were delivered and protected from the Egyptian army when God parted the Red Sea. Lot, his daughter and guests were delivered from a homosexual mob of rapist killers. King David's whole family and his soldiers were all rescued from a large raiding party of brigand soldiers, and David got back everything that had been stolen, plus the possessions of the raiding party. King David himself was also protected many times from death at the hands of King Saul's soldiers and from many other kings and tribal leaders and their soldiers. Abraham and his wife, Sarah, were delivered many times from their enemies, usually armed and fully trained soldiers. These are just a few examples from the Old Testament.

Question: You may ask, What about us today? We live in New Testament times. Do the covenant promises apply to us?

Answer: Yes, absolutely. We have a new and better covenant.

Question: Can we name any New Testament people whom God delivered and defended because they knew they had angelic protection?

Answer: Yes, absolutely! Jesus Himself, who for approximately thirty-three years was protected from the most dangerous threats of physical attacks again and again until He chose to lay down His life. On one occasion the apostles Peter and John were freed from jail by an angel of the Lord; see Acts 5: 17-20. Then there was Barnabas, whom God delivered simply by warning him to flee the city of Iconium because there was a plot to have him beaten and then stoned to death (see Acts 14: 2–7).

Question: What is God's will then concerning our lives, and what does He want us to do, die for Him or live for Him?

Answer: Live for Him! This is so we can be alive to receive the promises of Abraham, all of them, and use those blessings to bring others to know Jesus as their Lord and Saviour. Do you see it? I pray you do. God wants you alive so you can be blessed and be a blessing to others and share Jesus with them. The devil wants you to believe you have no protection against men or circumstances. He wants you dead so that you have no impact on the lives of others and tell no one about Jesus. If the devil could (he can't, but if he could), he would kill all believers in Christ now, so that no unbelievers could ever come to know Jesus.

Romans 10: 17 says, "Faith comes by hearing and hearing by the Word of God." *So how could anyone have faith in Christ if they have never heard the gospel?*

How could they hear if all God's people were dead? They could not, it's impossible. For that reason, the Bible says that God wants you to have life and have it more abundantly. Hallelujah, Jesus! He chose to die in our place so we could live to carry on His work or mission, which is to bless all the families of the earth. The wealth God wants us to have is to confirm or establish His promises, His covenant, for the benefit of all the families on earth, which he promised to Abraham and his Seed. That's Jesus and you, if you are in Christ. It's through Abraham that the Seed (singular), who is Jesus, would come, and anyone in Christ Jesus is also Abraham's seed and heir to the promise of God: to bless all the families of the earth, both physically (financially) and spiritually (in leading them to Jesus). Deuteronomy 8: 17–18 says God has given His people power to get wealth to confirm (as a sign of God's promise) the covenant that God made with Abraham and his Seed and his descendants in Christ.

Angels are sent by God to protect you and help you as you live your Christian life of service to God and others. God will command them to watch over you and your house in all your ways (at all times, in all places). See how the promises are linked together like an orderly chain? You need Jesus and forgiveness. You need to be baptized in Jesus' name, both in the Spirit and water; then you become a child of God and an heir with Christ of the promises. Then you learn more and more promises. You believe them, and you confess them over your life and your house. You receive them by faith and then actually see them in the natural world coming to pass in your life and your house, providing opportunity for great testimonies as to what God has done. Now you can teach others how to receive the same blessings you have. It's a chain reaction. You share the good news with others because you know the Word of God is good news.

Let's look at protection in Psalm 121: 1–8 (NIV):

> I (you) lift up my eyes to the hills –
>> where does my help come from?
> My help comes from the Lord,
>> the Maker of heaven and earth.
> He will not let your foot slip –
>> He who watches over you will not slumber;
> indeed, He who watches over Israel
>> will neither slumber nor sleep.
> The Lord watches over you –
>> the Lord is your shade at your right hand;
> the sun will not harm you by day (no harm comes in daylight)
>> nor the moon by night
>> (no harm comes to you at night, or in darkness).
> *The Lord will keep you from all harm –*
>> He will watch over your life;
> the Lord will watch over your coming (in) and going (out)
>> both *now and forevermore.*

These promises are written to you in Christ, Abraham's Seed. Jesus is the Seed, so you're the seed of Abraham. *No harm will befall you, none*, because the Lord promises to keep you away from it again and again! Traditions of people and churches say harm will come! God says, No, none, no harm will befall or come to you! So by faith in God and His promise, say aloud daily, "In the name of Jesus, by the blood of the Lamb, I have a covenant with the Almighty, which says no harm will come near me or my house. In accordance with Psalm 91: 10, I say of the Lord Jesus, He is God, my God, His Father is my Father, He is my refuge, my fortress in whom I trust, saying, no harm will befall me or my house, my family, or my goods (belongings), because He, God, will command His angels concerning me, to watch over me and guard me in all my ways. He will lift me up and make sure my foot does not even strike against a stone."

Say it, believe it, and receive it. You will see, you will experience the manifestation in your life. In addition, say aloud, "Lord, keep me and my house, my family, in exactly the right places at the right times and out of the wrong places at the wrong times, never being harmed or cursed, always being blessed and prospered, always being a great blessing to others, leading them to Jesus with the right words." Say this daily, based on your faith in the blood covenant promises of protection. Do not let anyone at any time talk you out of it, and you shall live and not die.

You must understand, your words matter very much in issues of life and death because life and death lie in the power of the tongue (see Prov. 18: 21). *God has revealed this in His Word.* God protects his people in limitless ways, including angels guarding you and God Himself protecting you; He can cause you to walk through a crowd of enemies, or He can transport you instantly from one place to another, to any distance from your attackers. He can send someone to warn you, "Do not go there." If He says this to you, do not disobey Him; take the warning! Do not go, no matter what! Go another day or another way! Ask God to reveal it to you. He will. He can keep you always in exactly the right places at the right time and out of the wrong places at the wrong times, never being harmed. Ask God to do this for you every day, morning and night. This is the best kind of protection, always being in exactly the right places at exactly the right times, God's planned times for you. Can you see it? Prevention is better than cure.

The best advice I can give is, once you pray that prayer in faith, be sensitive to what the Holy Spirit says. You need to have an inner prompting or inner knowing, accompanied by an inner peace of spirit or heart to know you're okay to go here or there at a given time. However, if you don't have inner peace about going somewhere, or if you don't have inner peace to go at that time, *do not go!* Go at a different time or go on a different route. Just say, "Lord, speak; reveal to me where I should go today, and where I should I be." Don't be rigid or stiff in your heart or in your thinking and will. Be soft or flexible, pliable like putty or plasticine, easy to shape, mould, or direct.

In Colossians 3: 15 and Philippians 4: 6–7, the Greek word translated *peace* means that His peace is "your umpire". It's easy once you get the hang of knowing God's voice or prompting inside; it's always accompanied by a deep inner peace. One of the best ways to hear from God about protection (or about anything, for that matter is to pray in tongues, to pray in the Spirit. Let the tongues, your God-given heavenly prayer language, come out of your mouth until you stop – don't stop yourself; just let it stop naturally – and then start singing in tongues. Sometimes you start to laugh in the Spirit. These signs of suddenly stopping or singing after your prayer in tongues or laughing after your prayer in tongues means it's done, it's complete, it is finished, and all is okay. Then just say, "Lord, what did You just tell me? Reveal it to me", and He will.

From 1 Corinthians 14: 13–15 we understand that this gift is called "interpretation of tongues" (*tongues* means your God-given gift of speaking in a language unknown to you, which comes out of your spirit, *not* out of your head or mind). Speaking in tongues is something that is not learned with the mind or at school or through study. It's a gift of the Holy Spirit, as seen in Mark 16: 17. It's a gift which can bring answers, knowledge, and protection as God reveals things to you from within your spirit, where His Spirit lives or dwells. You and He are one. He is in you.

If you don't yet speak in tongues or you're not yet baptised in the Holy Spirit, then all you need to do is ask. Luke 11: 13 says so. A suggested prayer is, "Father, I have asked Jesus into my heart, and now I ask You to baptise me in the Holy Spirit and Your power. Give me my gift of tongues, my heavenly language to speak and pray and sing in, amen. I receive it now by faith."

It may sound as if I'm off the track of protection, but I'm not. This praying and speaking in tongues is part of the armour of God referred to in Ephesians 6: 10–18. Some Christians don't realize praying in the Spirit (see key verse 18) is part of the armour, and they stop at verse 17. But in Greek, the sentences here flow into each other. The verse numbers were only inserted by the Bible translators for reference purposes so we can more easily find passages. This is a good tool or idea, but once you've found your Bible passage always remember that the original Hebrew and Greek flow constantly, one sentence into another. The chapter and verse divisions added later by translators restrict the flow in the original Hebrew and Greek. This is because each sentence depends upon the preceding sentence and the sentence following for its complete significance; all are part of the same message right through the Bible!

So verses 10–17 here are linked with verse 18. Armour does what? It protects: a helmet, a breastplate, a belt, a shield, a sword, armoured shoes, and finally, praying and interceding in the Spirit. First Corinthians 14: 2 tells us plainly that when you pray or speak in an unknown tongue, you pray with your spirit and speak or communicate to God, speaking directly to His Spirit from your spirit. This is Spirit to spirit, knowledge revealed direct from God, not knowledge you have learned at college or school.

Please catch the next few pages, but make sure what you think you hear lines up with God's Word, God's commands, God's promises. The Holy Spirit will never, ever tell you to do anything that is not written, commanded, or promised in God's Word, the Bible. He only ever tells you to do what is right, good, correct, and kind. If you ever hear a thought telling you to kill someone, steal from someone, cheat someone, be unkind, or break any of God's commands, just say *no*, and don't do it! Recognise that these thoughts are from the enemy. You must grasp that, but fear not! Just keep reading your Bible each day, and little by little you will learn more and more of God's ways, commands, and promises. The only way to be certain of what exact or precise truth is, is to accept only God's written Word as your blueprint and guideline for your thoughts and actions towards other people.

Praying in tongues *must* be accompanied by reading God's Word daily. I encourage you to spend at least half an hour a day; this really should be your minimum time spent reading as an investment in your personal spiritual growth. Keep trusting in the blood covenant God made between you and Jesus, knowing you've inherited the promised will of God that's written down for you in the Bible, your own personal copy of God's Will and Testament or Covenant.

This faith in Jesus is really faith in Him as the final blood sacrifice presented by God the Father. As you can see from Romans 3: 25, we partake in the benefits of the New Covenant through faith in His blood sacrifice. Do you see where your trust for protection comes from? You trust because Jesus shed His blood, being the final sacrifice, and your believing this causes God to count you as righteous, righteous enough to give you freely all the Abrahamic promises that Jesus had and that Jesus now gives freely to you. Check out Galatians 3: 29 again: "And if you are Christ's, you are Abraham's seed and heirs according to the promise." God agreed to this and signed the agreement (sealed the covenant) in blood, meaning God can do nothing other than protect you. God gives protection freely, as a free gift. So your faith for protection comes by believing God's written Word, which says you are freely justified by God; you are counted righteous by Him through faith in Jesus' blood.

This is the New Testament, people – God's Word, God's written Will saying, "Have faith in the blood God shed, his own blood, in Christ." You inherit the promises, including protection, now. Reader, you have to choose whether or not to carry on reading and studying the promises and covenants of God. Just be quiet; don't argue, but ask the Holy Spirit to show you all things, about how you should interpret and understand God's Word, especially the commands, promises, and covenant blood agreements in Christ. You will find that all I have written is knowledge revealed exactly to us by God the Holy Spirit for our benefit –yours, dear reader, and mine. This is the same Holy Spirit who Jesus promised would teach us all things, lead us into all truth, reveal to us things yet to come, and show that all things are possible.

It takes us humans time to learn and time to understand everything the Holy Spirit wants to show us. I don't yet know all about every subject on earth or in the universe, let alone the whole knowledge of God, but this knowledge is being increased week by week, month by month, year by year. This is for all believers who choose to be quiet and study the Word of God and ask the Holy Spirit to reveal to them the precise meaning of what they are reading and studying. Then and only then will you learn the truth that the promises are yours. More importantly, you will start believing them and start receiving the benefits of all God promises you. You will be glad and rejoice as you learn more, know and understand more deeply, and rest on an unshakeable faith in God through His love and the blood of Jesus, that He will do for you everything that He promised, everything!

God wants to reveal His truth to you more than you want to learn, no matter how hungry you are to learn. God is hungrier to unfold for you every aspect of His Word and your covenant in Jesus Christ. God loves us from His depths to our depths and simply wants the best for us. The only way He could convince us to believe His covenant promises was to have them written out, swear by Himself that He would give them freely to us, and then sign the page with His own signature in His own precious lifeblood, and then die. He took upon himself all the curses of the Law, all the sickness and diseases, all sin and wrong, all the dying, all the poverty, all the misery, all the depression. He shed His blood and rose again triumphant, utterly defeating all that Satan threw at Him, to rescue and bless humanity and to carry out what He had promised.

Hallelujah, what love. Thank God I am learning more day by day, and I believe and accept it all, even though at present I don't fully understand it. Nevertheless, the Holy Spirit has been sent to teach me all things about God, His love, His Word, and His promises. Rejoice that we now live in a time when more and more revelation of God's Word has been given to us and is actually increasing steadily. We can put on the TV and tune in to ten or more anointed Christian channels with great Holy Spirit–filled teachers to explain more and more about Jesus and His Word, commands, and promises. I respectfully but urgently ask you to consider obtaining cable or satellite TV or radio which airs anointed Bible teachers 24/7. Praise God, what a blessed time we live in. There are many gospel tools and Spirit-filled teachers to help us understand, but it's up to us to tune in and listen daily as well as spending time studying the Bible in our own home, not just at church.

Let's get hungry for God and spend time with Him. Amen! The only reason people don't fully understand the Scriptures today is that we have had so much help from doubters and unbelieving Bible scholars telling us that God didn't really mean for us to be protected in health and financially blessed. They say healing passed away with the death of the first apostles. We began to believe their interpretation of the Bible instead of taking daily quality time ourselves to study it and pray for God's wisdom, knowledge, and revelation so we might fully understand. Yet, praise God, things have changed; Bibles flood the earth, and Spirit-filled believers who know God and His Word in truth and Spirit flood the earth, and we are growing in numbers daily! Satan is afraid, make no mistake! For the first time in history those in the body of Christ, the church, are learning who they are in Christ and the power and authority that is theirs through the great and precious promises by which we participate in the divine nature of God – and guess what: miracles have started up again.

Supernatural, godly provision is back again. Believers expect healthy bodies all their lives and long life. Just like the New Testament disciples, saints are laying their hands on the sick in Jesus' name and seeing them get well instantly or recover by faith in Jesus over a period of time. Praise God, believers are seeing that they have protection from God personally and from angels, their guardian angels. Just like the Old Testament believers, knowledge of the covenant promises is being restored on planet Earth. Praise God!

Reader, if you are one of the unbelievers, black or white, Muslim or Hindu, or a follower of any belief or any religion, atheist, evolutionist, etc. – repent now! *Turn now to God and say, "Jesus, I cry out to you. Come into my life and save me now! I accept that You died for me so I will not go into the lake of fire, the second death. I accept that You shed your blood for me. Make me now a new creation by Your Holy Spirit coming to live in my heart. I want the new birth, to be born again, Amen."* If you do this, you are what the Bible calls "saved", and hallelujah, you become a joint heir with Jesus of all God's promises, including the total forgiveness of all sin.

~ ~ ~

As I close, here are a variety of God's promises of protection for you to believe and say each day until faith rises up in your heart and you know, because you know that you know, that protection is yours every day.

Readers, this, I believe, is the best and most powerful confession and protection prayer. Say this aloud every day: "Father, in the name of Jesus I pray, keep me and my family (name your family members) in exactly the right places at the right times and always out of the wrong places at the wrong times, always being blessed and being a blessing to others and never being harmed or cursed and never harming or cursing others. Keep me always telling others about Jesus, and send the right people to me who will accept Jesus through me. Give the right words for me to speak, and empower me with Your mighty anointing to do mighty works and miracles, for Your glory. Thank you, Lord. I believe now, as I pray, that I have what I say because Jesus, the Seed of Abraham said so in Mark 11: 22–24. Amen, praise Jesus!"

This, brothers and sisters in the Lord, is better than having to be delivered from harm by angels or God himself. You only need to be delivered from harm because you are in the wrong place at the wrong time with the wrong people or in the wrong circumstances. It's always better to be in the right place at the right time. Angels and the Lord will protect you from the most impossible circumstances. He promised it, but you won't need it if you are in the right place at the right time. My advice is to confess it daily and believe it daily.

Declare this aloud: "I have been given power and authority. Jesus gave it to me. So angels, ministering spirits, all of you sent for me, go in Jesus' name, and protect me and my family and our belongings at all places and at all times. I thank Jesus for you, angels, for serving and obeying God and serving and obeying me because I speak God's Word and promises. God promised me that you are sent for me, the heir of salvation in Christ Jesus. Make straight the crooked path; go before us and go with us, now and always and as God declares in Psalm 121: 7, no harm will befall me, my wife, my children, my family. I believe it and expect it, thanks be to Jesus and His shed blood of the New Covenant.

"Lord, in Psalm 103: 20–21 Your Word says that Your angels are mighty ones who do Your bidding and obey Your Word. So, Father, as Jesus has given me all authority to speak Your Word, I fully expect in faith that the angels sent for me, an heir of salvation, have to obey Your word coming out of my mouth.

"Father, in Mark 11: 22–24, Jesus said that if I speak to a mountain and say, 'Be cast into the sea', and do not doubt His Word in my heart, it shall be done! I shall have whatsoever I say. I say, in Jesus' name, I'm blessed, and I'm protected. I say in Jesus' name, angels, my guardians, go. I commission you, watch over us night and day. Hallelujah, Jesus!"

Say this aloud: "Father, in Psalm 106: 8–12, You said You saved Your people for Your name's sake. I come to you now in Jesus' name, the name above all names; do for me now what You did for them. You made Your mighty power known. You rebuked the Red Sea, and it dried up. You led Your people through the depths of the sea on a dry path like desert sand. You saved Your people from the hand of the enemy and redeemed them. The waters of the Red Sea covered their enemies (the Egyptian army), and not one of them survived. Your people believed Your promises of protection, and they sang Your praises, but they forgot that You saved them and forgot Your word and promises. In Jesus' name, I will not forget You or Your promises. I will spend time studying Your Word daily. Help me do this, Lord, in Jesus' name, in His power.

"So I fully expect, Lord, that as an heir of salvation and heir of angels protecting me, all of the ministering angels, spirits sent specifically for me, Lord, in Jesus' name, I claim it: Do for me what you promised them and did for them. Save and protect me and my house from the hand of the enemy – from men, women, demons, animals, and all danger and evil – and I also will sing Your praises. Jesus, I believe Your promises of protection. They were made to You, and I'm in You. You said if I am in You, I am an heir to the promise. Thank You for dying for me and shedding Your precious blood for me. I accept the blood covenant which You cannot break."

Pray this, all readers: "Father, in Jesus' name show me daily in Your Word as I read and study more of the protection promises in both the Old and New Testaments. According to Mark 11: 22–24, because I believed, I received protection when I prayed. I also believe You will give me wisdom and revealed knowledge of more protection promises according to James 1: 5–8. If I ask for wisdom (revelation, knowledge given by the Holy Spirit explaining what God's Word really means and how to exactly interpret it), it will be given, and I will not doubt I have this wisdom to know and find more and more promises about protection. Open my eyes, Lord. I believe I receive now. I know it will come, and as it is written, I have the mind of Christ. Also, according to James 5: 16, it's written that the prayer of the righteous makes much power available to them. I am the righteousness of God in Christ, cleansed of all sin by His blood covenant. Therefore, I expect great knowledge and faith in the promises and faith in Your ability to perform those promises of protection in my life and my family's lives. I am not a doubter; I am a believer. I will receive from you, Jesus. Amen."

Now, reader, remember: faith comes, increases, grows, by hearing audibly God's Word. Go to a church where there are men and women of God who truly understand His Word and can teach you faith. Love the Lord your God (Yahweh, who is Jesus) with all your heart, soul, mind, and strength. Love your neighbour as Jesus loved you. All the law and the prophets hang on these two commands. If you love God and your brothers in Christ, indeed anyone, then you will not cheat them, steal from them, deceive them, or hurt them. You will not commit adultery or bear false witness. That's why Jesus gave you a new, born-again recreated spirit. It's a heart issue to love God and others. God has created a new heart within you. If you have truly asked Jesus into your life, you have the love of God in your heart now, so let it out!

Allow the Holy Spirit to guide your every thought and action. As James 1: 22–25 says, don't only listen to God's Word or just read it, but do what it says, and then you will be blessed (prospered in health, wealth, and protection) in all you do. Don't you want that? Yes.

Amen, come, Lord Jesus. Tell others the good news. Isn't it good that our God is a good God all the time? Love Jesus. Keep His Word. Love your brothers and sisters in Christ. Love all people. Be a blessing. Be a light for Christ in a dark world. Speak God's truth in love as you have opportunity. Be strong in the Lord.

Through us, the seed of Abraham – that's what we are in Christ Jesus – all the earth shall be blessed. This gospel shall be heard all over the earth as a witness to all peoples, and only then will the end come, the end of darkness and demon rule. King Jesus will return to rule on a new earth with his new race of born-again people. Amen and amen! Thanks be to God. Our God is an awesome God. He reigns! Let Him reign in your life, your mind, your heart, and your spirit. *Amen.*

TESTIMONIES FROM JOHN

There are many testimonies which could be shared of John's experiences. The following are just a few examples of the faithfulness of God.

Concerning Finance

On one occasion, whilst John was going through a particularly bad time, God had prompted him to give away some money that he had saved for a much-needed holiday. "Now what shall I do, Lord?" he enquired. "Look in the hall" was the Lord's prompting. This he did, without finding anything. "Look in the hall," the Lord told him again and added "You are not looking carefully enough." So John searched more carefully and moved the phone off the shelf. As he did so, he found a sealed envelope with these words written on it: "From heaven's bank to John." It was full of twenty-pound notes which more than covered what he had given away.

Concerning Healing

Over a period of many years John has seen healings and miracles breaking out after the preaching and teaching of the Word of God. Numerous people have come to him and expressed their need for healing in their bodies. John has taught them how to believe God to meet that need based upon the promises in the Word of God, and they have been healed of many diseases including epilepsy, physical blockages, and cancers, including lung cancers diagnosed and seen on x-rays which later were shown to have disappeared completely without treatment. On many occasions people have wanted to see healing, but John has taught them not only to receive the healing that they needed at the time but also how to live in the abundance of health that is learned by reading the direct words of Jesus.

Concerning Provision

John was working in the North of England, witnessing in the whole area, leading many people to the Lord, and teaching them the principles of Scripture, including that of provision. One lady was desperately poor and needed a washing machine. John asked her, "Do you believe God will provide?" just as he was leaving to go home. The lady said she did believe. John set off home and five minutes later someone asked him whether he needed a washing machine. On hearing that he did, he gave John the machine, which he then arranged to be delivered and fitted for her into her kitchen. As a result, she was saved and born again. Another friend had lots of dogs and needed a fridge. She had been told, "God doesn't give you things", so John prayed with her. The next day she was offered a fridge, which John fitted for her. On seeing what had happened, another friend said that she also needed a fridge, and two days later John was passing a house with a fridge outside the door. The householder offered it to John, again free of charge. All these stories of provision point to the fact of John being in the right place at the right time and always blessed to be a blessing, based on Genesis 12: 2 and Mark 11: 22.

Concerning Protection

On a research visit, to a foreign country where it was hard to find the historical information that John required for his biblical studies, he had spent some time in a certain place which was difficult of access to foreign nationals. It was quite late when he left, and as he walked away from the building, he encountered a very threatening group of people barring his way. Quickly he prayed for guidance; he spoke out loud and bound Satan in Jesus' name over the situation, and the Holy Spirit showed him a picture of Jesus walking through the mob that took Him to the top of the cliff to throw Him off. When Jesus got to the top He walked straight through the crowd. The Lord showed John to do the same, so he walked towards the group, and they parted and let him through.

Concerning Provision

Running Bible groups for the poorest members of John's local community in the North of England was a very costly business. Drug addicts' children were suffering under their parents' lifestyle, so food had to be bought for them. So much was needed that John's own family often seemed likely to be short of necessities, but they prayed and spoke to remind the Lord that it said in His Word, "Give and it shall be given unto you; good measure, pressed down, and shaken together, and running over shall be given unto you" (Luke 6: 38). They had no food, but they had faith, and they had a faithful God. John asked his wife to write a list of what they needed. Then God spoke to John and told him on his evening run to run up into the hills instead of his usual route. So he did, and at the end of his run, by the bus stop was a bag of groceries, and in that bag was all that they needed. This continued for two months until one day at the end of that period someone came and promised them a regular weekly income, eventually amounting to several thousand pounds. The miracle provision of food stopped the same day the promise of ongoing finance was given.

Opportunities

For many years there have been opportunities to bring the gospel to others, and John has taken each one as people have been hungry to hear the message of salvation. As in Jesus' day, there has also been opposition, and when young men have been listening, many times there have been those within the group he has spoken to who do not want to hear and have tried to dissuade their friends from listening. This strength of reaction has grown considerably during recent months. However John's teaching groups have grown and have gone from strength to strength. People are coming to faith in Christ and are being discipled, including people of the established denominations.

Printed in Great Britain
by Amazon